D1596459

NAKED IS THE BEST DISGUISE

NAKED IS THE BEST DISGUISE

My Life as a Stripper

Lauri Lewin

WILLIAM MORROW AND COMPANY, INC.
NEW YORK   1984

Aside from myself, the people in this book are
composites. Their identifying characteristics and their
names have been changed to protect their privacy.
The events all occurred but in the lives of more
people than I present.

L.L.

Library of Congress Cataloging in Publication Data .

Lewin, Lauri.
  Naked is the best disguise.

  1. Lewin, Lauri. 2. Strip-teasers—United States—
Biography. I. Title.
PN1949.S7L4 1984   792.7'028'0924 [B]   83-25117
ISBN 0-688-02929-9

Printed in the United States of America

First Edition

1 2 3 4 5 6 7 8 9 10

BOOK DESIGN BY PATRICE FODERO

for my parents

ACKNOWLEDGMENTS

The community of women of which I feel a part has in many ways shaped this book. First and foremost are the strippers who spoke to me with candor and depth about their lives. They showed me a beauty invisible to most people who view strippers. I wrote this book in the hope that more such women would survive to speak out about what they've seen. My women writers' group continues to provide me with support and camaraderie. The feminists, whose works and ideas have contributed to my understanding of pornography, stripping, and myself as a woman in America, are too numerous to list here. Let me say that Susan Griffin's *Pornography and Silence* touched me deeply, as did the writings of Angela Davis, Tillie Olsen, and Adrienne Rich. Linda Gordon, professor of history at the University of Massachusetts at Boston, profoundly influenced my thinking about gender, class, and history.

I am also indebted to the men—customers, agents, bartenders, club owners and managers—who shared with me their impressions of the strip joint.

Anne Froines, Jean Humez, Pancho Savery, and Eileen Wiznitzer, of the University of Massachusetts, and Mary Nash, of the Radcliffe Institute, helped me enormously with their critiques of the manuscript at various points. Ron Schreiber, of U-Mass/Boston, and Barbara Starrett, of Beacon College, were the first to encourage me to write about stripping. Early on in the project, Lynn Conroy taught me the value of networking. Dean James Curran, of John Jay College, went out of his way to discuss my book with me.

To the many people who read and commented on the manuscript, and to those who believed in me even when I didn't, I wish to express my gratitude: Bruce Fieldman, Carlos and Myra Fraga-Diaz, Abra Glenn-Allen, Pauline Goodman, Lisa Handwerker, Nancy Koch, Bill Kornfeld, Diana Lett, Henry Lieberman, Tommy Magee, Lillian Miller, Larry Mitchell, Lenore Monroe, Andy Nash, Roy Nordblom, Bamidele Osumarea, Jan Park, Dawna Provost, Faith Snow, Claudia Sperber, Mark Weiss, Liz Westerfield, Libby Zimmerman, and Lucy Johnson Zweibel.

My father, mother, stepfather, sisters, and brother have been generous with their insights and their love. Friend, mentor, and also family, Leslie Jean Roberts has stuck by me through some very tough times. To all of these people I am deeply grateful.

Bertell Ollman provided the clue that got the project rolling. Katinka Matson, my agent, has been enthusiastic from the start. James Landis, my editor at Morrow, brought great skill and sensitivity to this book; he was a joy to work with. Mina Lupone did a superb job of typing the first draft.

Finally, I want to thank Carroy U. Ferguson, who has been a companion in the fullest sense of the word. He has shown me that I can trust again.

CONTENTS

No mask like open truth to cover lies,
As to go naked is the best disguise.

—WILLIAM CONGREVE
The Double Dealer

ONE

SO GRACEFUL,
THE CLASSICAL DANCE

By 1979, I had worked in Boston's Combat Zone for three years. On my way to work, I passed signs that advertised "XXX Movies," "Exotic Dancers," and an "All-Nude College Girl Revue." In the Zone, hookers paced the streets, while johns ate at pizza counters. Pimps gathered at the corners to display their hats and gold and cars and women. I'd once seen a group of young hoods form a circle around a child prostitute, taunting, "Come on, baby, give us some for free." "Oh, no," she'd fired, hands on hips, her body tilted on five-inch heels, "you've got to pay." In front of the Puritan porno theater, once the glory of burlesque, there'd stood a one-legged man with his pants down around his knee. "I'm gonna get them Vietcong," he'd yelled. "I'm gonna shoot me some tonight." I'd seen two cops get out of their cruiser to question an elderly Chinese man who did not speak English; they'd told him his rights and slammed him against a brick wall.

Each day, before noon, I'd step over the sleeping drunks on the sidewalks. I'd see dancers from all the strip joints on their way to work: getting out of cabs, kissing boyfriends good-bye, rushing from the subway. Dancers who did not work regularly at any one particular club carried suitcases full of costumes. Some of the women fit the popular image of the stripper: heavily made-up, wearing tight pants and spiked heels, they strutted confidently into the bars. Others, wearing blue jeans and carrying knapsacks, could not be distinguished from the many college students in Boston. At work, the differences between the women blurred. They all donned the stripper's uniform of bra and G-string.

I worked the day shift at the Nudie-Tease Nightclub. It allowed me the time to live my double life. In the mornings I'd attend classes at the university; in the afternoons I'd strip. The day shift was calmer. While a steady stream of customers kept business going, we rarely had a full house. Men tended to drink less when they had to return to work in an hour. Fewer dancers believed that they'd make a quantum leap from the Nudie-Tease to Hollywood. At night, the club became crowded. Some men drank too much, yelled obscenities at the dancers, and ended up on the street with their heads bleeding. Many dancers on the night shift believed in the myth of the show girl; they competed fiercely for top billing, spent thousands of dollars on costumes, and insisted that the bouncers eject any man who shouted obscenities.

On first glance, the Nudie-Tease could have been any other nightclub with live entertainment. Its walls were black and lined with mirrors, its barstools red. A long T-shaped runway ran waist level to the bartenders. I could imagine a country western singer up there professing her love for her rugged cowboy, or a troupe of tap dancers softshoeing to "Tea for Two." The finer details of the bar belied that fantasy. On one wall hung glossy photographs of the club's feature attractions, young women wearing meager costumes. Several steps led down to a smaller, more intimate barroom, where only a raised strip of wood separated the bar from the stage. A sign identified that room as the "Bare Beaver Bar."

14

In the mornings, before the lights were dimmed, the male employees starred. Bartenders, dressed in the formal black and white attire of their trade, whisked wet rags across the already clean counters. They stocked their bars with beer, then filled empty liquor bottles with the water, tea, and juice used for dancers' drinks later in the day. The porter mopped the stages and wiped fingerprints off the mirrors. He dotingly dusted off the photographs on the wall. In the dressing room, he made piles of the refuse left by dancers from the night before: crusty G-strings, feather boas, crushed beer cans. The manager scheduled shows and bragged about the brawl and the broad he'd had the night before. Behind the one-way mirror in his office, the owner of the Nudie-Tease watched over his club.

By 1979, I thought that nothing in the Zone could surprise me. But the people sitting across from me in the Nudie-Tease one day caught my attention.

They were an unusual sight in the Combat Zone: an elderly couple, huddled together in a booth, both drinking orange juice. They looked like they were dressed for church. He wore a pressed, faded black suit. She fingered her crucifix. I watched him turn his head back and forth to follow the dancer up and down the runway. When she bent over, he cocked his head to the side. When she rolled on the floor, he smiled rapturously. Then I looked at the old woman. She, too, turned her head back and forth, but in the opposite direction, to avoid looking at the dancer. Occasionally, unsmiling, she glanced over at the old man.

I went over to their booth. "Are you enjoying the show?" I asked.

"Very beautiful," he said with a thick Italian accent.

"Do you like it?" I asked the woman.

"My husband, he wants to see." She shook her head.

"And you came with him?"

"Of course. My husband."

He tore his eyes away from the stage. "My wife," he presented her to me. "Beautiful!" His eyes had focused on my chest. "You dance?" I nodded. He turned to his wife. "Like our Rosa. Little girl."

She smiled for the first time. "You want to sit?"

"For a minute. I have to dance soon." I didn't want them to have to buy a drink for me; they looked poor.

We talked for several minutes. They were in their mid-seventies. During their ten years in America, they had rarely ventured beyond the Italian North End of Boston. She had rarely gone out of the house and her English was poor. They had seven children and eighteen grandchildren. What were they doing in the Combat Zone?

"Beautiful," he repeated, this time clearly intent upon the nude woman on the stage.

The old woman blushed. "This is the first time. He never sees."

"He never sees strippers?" I asked.

"Woman. He never sees a woman."

"You've never seen a woman?" I asked him, not believing. He shook his head no. "Your wife? You've seen your wife." Again, he shook his head. "How many years have you been married?"

"We're married forty-eight years." He patted her plump arm.

"I don't know," she said. "He wants to see. I come with him." She looked bewildered but resigned to accept her husband's curiosity, his new privilege as an American. I wondered if these ten minutes of visible nudity would obscure for him forty-eight years of loving her in the dark.

They left the Nudie-Tease when the dance ended. Using her husband's arm as a crutch, the old woman limped badly.

I tried to imagine my own grandmother in the Combat Zone. I pictured her, robust and determined, pushing her way through the crowd of men at the Nudie-Tease. From the stage, I would see her. She'd be wearing a simple cotton dress. Under

16

her arm, clutched tightly, would be her black purse, full of treasures: pictures of all the grandchildren, her Social Security card, my first poem, and bunches of tissues. She'd grab a handful of tissues and stride right up to the stage, where I'd be rolling around nude on the bare wooden planks. "Lauri," she would ask, "is it clean, that floor? Don't catch cold." With deft movements, she'd wipe off the stage as if it were any other surface.

But that would not have been her reaction. My grandmother would never go into a strip joint. Sex had been a brief, distasteful part of her life. She married late and divorced quickly. My mother, the only child of that marriage, grew up without a father. In Grandma's view, men could be loved as human beings capable of creating art or poetry, but as virile beings they only caused pain. She longed for a male companion, someone to engage in an exchange of ideas; the touching of bodies, the invasion of privacy, that accompanied such a relationship, repulsed her.

Like the Italian couple, my grandmother was an immigrant. She came here as a teenager in the early part of the century, one of thousands of Jews who left Russia to escape the pogroms. For forty years, she worked in a factory, always sorry that she had given up a chance to become a schoolteacher. She prided herself on being one of the fastest button sewers in her union, yet she constantly fought against defining herself by that job. Finally, in her old age, she was able to devote herself to her studies. Like a scribe, she spent her days copying into notebooks the words of other writers.

When I was young, Grandma was my companion. My father complained that she kept me hidden in the back room of the apartment. There, she told me wildly romanticized stories about her childhood in Russia. The flowers talked to the bees, the Jews talked to the gentiles, and travelers from Palestine stopped by for dinner in the evening. Although I knew that she

17

omitted the harsher realities from her reminiscences, such as the times when her entire *shtetl* hid in cellars to escape the violence of the Cossacks, I loved the world she created. It smelled like the rising dough of her cinnamon cake. It blunted the sounds of my parents' arguing in the next room. Even if my parents divorced, I could retreat to safety in this inner room of Grandma's world.

My parents did divorce, when I was almost four years old. My older sister Nina and I stayed with our mother, who soon remarried. My stepfather, an activist in the civil rights and peace movements of the 1960's, took a teaching job at a small black college in the South. By then a family of six, we left New York. Atheist by practice, we nonetheless became Jews living among Christians; we looked different. While our neighbors protested school desegregation and voted for George Wallace, we slipped out to Washington to march in protest of their views.

As different as I felt from other kids, I wanted to be accepted by them. I rarely defended my parents' views in public. During the morning prayers in school, I pretended to be pious. If friends came to visit, I turned my parents' books around on the bookshelves, although I was probably the only ten-year-old in my school who knew enough about Karl Marx to recognize the danger. Associating curly hair with Jewishness or blackness, I straightened my hair; when it rained and my hair became curly again, I refused to leave the house.

At the same time, I valued certain aspects of my differentness. I wanted to be the smartest kid in the class. When, around the age of eleven or so, it became fashionable for girls to play dumb, I couldn't bring myself to do it. I wanted to look pretty on the outside, get the rings, attention, and status of the popular girls, and still be smart on the inside. Other people in my family led double lives. Why couldn't I? My stepfather maintained a middle-class facade while he agitated against the government. My grandmother had worked in a factory while

18

secretly pursuing her studies. It was difficult but necessary, I believed, to live with a tension between one's real self and what one must do to survive.

That's why I thought Grandma would understand my stripping. I'd tried to tell her about it on my last visit home.

"You know what I do for work, Grandma? I stand on a stage and take off my clothes."

"You're a fashion model?"

"Not exactly. Models keep their clothes on; I take mine off. I'm a stripper. I dance."

"You dance! So graceful, the classical dance. I saw the ballet on the TV last night."

"No, no. How can I describe it? It's more like a prostitute."

"A prostitute!" She held her fingers up to her lips in a panic, then ran to make sure that the door was bolted.

"Not a prostitute. A show girl. Striptease."

Finally, a word she understood. "Ach, that business," she scowled. "Do you know that you are wasting a talented mind? You could go on to become a college professor, or a doctor."

"I'm just trying to survive," I said.

She waved away that explanation with an impatient flick of her wrist. "You girls, you've had too much freedom. What could we expect, a little girl on her own? You're not an adult. Oy, why did we let you go?" She began to protest in Yiddish. Then, calmer, she stroked my hair. I watched the loose flesh of her arm swing slowly back and forth. I hated the thought that my flesh would someday hang like that, and yet I wanted to curl up in her softness. "Lauri, darling," she began her offer, "I'll tell you something. You have a grandma who loves you very much. Anytime you want, you can come stay with me. I'll buy a fold-out bed, on payments, and you'll do whatever you want. I'll stay as quiet as a mouse in my room all day while you study. And you can entertain your little friends in the living room here, yes?"

"I can't. When you were young, that woman said you could

stay in her house while you studied, and you couldn't do it. You needed to be on your own, even though it meant working in the factory."

"That was the biggest mistake in my life. I could have been a *teacherin.*"

"I'm not a stripper! You were more than a button sewer. You made a separation. I can do it, too."

I couldn't tell her that I had a cocaine habit to feed. How would I explain the excitement I felt when a roomful of men applauded my body? She'd never understand if I said I felt guilty for being middle-class. If I told her I needed attention, she'd offer me hers, undivided. And why wasn't her attention enough for me anymore? I didn't know.

I said, "I'll quit soon. It's temporary."

I averted my eyes, because I knew that I had no intention of leaving my job. Stripping had been part of my life for over three years.

I was sixteen years old when I first entered the life in the Combat Zone. I was unprepared for what I saw, although I had flirted with sex, drugs, and the underworld before that. A peculiar set of circumstances made it possible for me, a middle-class high school student, to consider stripping.

When I was twelve years old, Nina and I went to New York to live with our father. Under political pressure, my stepfather had quit his teaching job in North Carolina. Anticipating the ordeal of unemployment, and realizing that the family couldn't depend on only one breadwinner, my mother had entered nursing school. She was in her mid-thirties at the time, with four kids at home. Tensions in the household escalated. The adults fought about politics and money; the kids fought for the attention of the adults. My father's periodic visits created an unprecedented fury. "He should pay child support instead of flying down here all the time," my mother would say. When Nina and I annoyed her, she'd threaten to send us to live with him. Finally, we took her up on her threat. She let us go because she saw no other solution. In her view, she gave up her right to influence us. She'd express regret for having made that decision in the years to come.

Nina and I moved up north to a father who had long hair, smoked marijuana, lived with his young girlfriend, and talked about sex often and openly. From his words and life-style, I gathered that sex was natural, necessary, and pleasurable. He told me it was okay to masturbate, and from then on I masturbated with more peace of mind. He brought me to parties where I learned to flirt with grown men. I found books on his bookshelves that celebrated touching, "sexual liberation," orgasms for everyone. I felt a great sense of relief to learn that my sex life would not always consist of silently masturbating under guilty sheets and passively waiting for boys to ask me to go steady. I could hardly wait to be old enough to emulate my father's life-style.

When I was fourteen, my father took a sabbatical from his teaching position in New York and we moved up to Cambridge, Massachusetts. Nina, who was then sixteen, spent the weekends camped out in our living room with her boyfriend. I envied her. I wanted a boyfriend who would think my body was grown-up enough to make love to, who would come faithfully to my door every Friday and stay until Sunday. I examined myself in the mirror. My hair, which I had braided, straightened and ironed since my childhood in the South, I now released into an afro. My breasts, I decided, were big enough to be let out of their padded bra. Most of all, I wanted to discard my innocence. I took the vibrator I found in my father's room into the bathroom, where I deliberately broke my hymen. I spent my afternoons in fantasies about the men who would take me to bed and make passionate love to me. I rehearsed endless variations of romantic scenes with handsome men. For instance, the man would say, "I love cherries." I would respond, "My favorite fruit is the banana." We would then run to the nearest bed and make love for hours. I spent my evenings surreptitiously reading books from my father's shelves. I traveled through nine hundred pages of the true, lurid accounts of a nineteenth-century gentleman's "frisky" adventures with housemaids, whores, and horny noblewomen. I memorized the entire contents of an explicit book entitled *Oragenitalism* and then practiced the techniques on the vibrator. I must have read *Lady Chatterly's Lover* ten times.

From what I could see, sex was sex. The more the better. I saw no difference between the sex my father had with his girlfriend and the sex I began to have with men I picked up in the park, on the subway, in the library. The more people I slept with the more sophisticated I would be. Sophistication opened up an adult world where I'd be free from the divisive and cruel games of high school sexuality: the competition, pressure, lying about what one did, and the rumors that resulted no matter what one did. I thought that promiscuity would enable me to pass into adulthood without having to suffer through adolescence.

The little my father knew about my activities disturbed him, but he didn't know how to stop me. He was afraid that any intervention on his part would send me running back to my mother. Perhaps he was afraid of losing my affection. I pushed and pushed him to see at what point he'd stand up and say, "I'm your parent, not just your friend, and you can't be doing what you're doing." I remember one time when I was about to leave the house dressed in almost nothing, with garish makeup smeared across my face. He finally said, "No, you can't go out looking like that." I gladly washed off the makeup and changed my clothes, relieved to have elicited his concern.

The following year, he returned to New York to teach. Nina and I refused to leave Boston. Tired of moving every year, we arranged to live with friends and their families in Brookline, an upper-middle-class suburb of Boston. What had been a relatively unstructured life with my father became a life devoid of any supervision. No one told me where to go or when to come home. Like many of the kids in my high school, I experimented with drugs, slept with boys, and worked for Horace.

Working for Horace was crucial in the development of the attitude that would enable me to work as a stripper a year later. He was a man in his late forties who owned an antique clothing store in the ghetto. Several young women from my school, including Nina, had worked for him. None of them stayed very long at the job, and they were all very quiet about why they quit. I began to work for him when I was fifteen.

Horace's nineteen-year-old girlfriend had been found dead in an alley; some people thought he had killed her. I don't know the truth of the situation. At the time, I added the possibility that he might be a murderer to a list of other criminal activities that went on in the store. The antique clothing store was a weak front for a bookie joint. Many drugs and much money exchanged hands in the store. Junkies and other down-and-out people came in to sell stolen goods. I had gone to work in this store to make a little pocket money, and to get some funky old velvet and lace dresses. Instead, I walked into the underworld. Everyone there seemed to hold a secret, to rush stealthily in and out of the store, and to speak in hushed tones. "I barely made it out of there alive, man, but I've got the stuff for you." They walked about with an air of self-importance, the wary pride of people who narrowly escape from disaster. These men were the heroes of the scenario; I did not know who the enemies were. The pace, the mystery, the foreignness of the place entranced me. The drugs with which Horace generously plied me kept me in a foggy, receptive state of mind. I was too fascinated to perceive that in this world where everyone lived on the edge, always in danger of losing their lives, I too was in danger.

Horace would ask me to model dresses for him. He insisted that these sheer, form-fitting dresses looked better with nothing underneath. If I was some uptight kid who was scared to be real, I could walk right out the door, he'd say. If I was ready to be a woman, to be proud of my beautiful body, I'd go put on the dress and show him how fine I looked. Anxious to be a "real woman," I obliged. It was almost like playing dress-up. I enjoyed the admiration of the men who came through the store.

When I was alone in the store with Horace, the game took on another dimension. He began to curse and "talk dirty" to me. He'd say, "Come on, baby, tell me how much you want this big, sweet cock. Tell me how bad you want it." He enjoyed my embarrassment. The talk was foreplay; he also abused me. He liked to stand behind the counter with his hands down my pants, and say to an unknowing customer, "May I help you?" Later he would masturbate in front of me. I let him do this; I came back to work every week.

Because I wanted the drugs, clothing, and excitement offered by the job, I learned to cope with its unpleasant elements. While Horace cursed and molested me, I would repeat over and over to myself, "This is not happening." I practiced the art of passivity. I could tolerate it if he touched or looked at me, but I would not touch him. This was my first inkling of what was to become a way of life for me when I became a stripper.

I got my first job as a stripper a year later. Nina had gone away to college in the Midwest. She did not lead a quiet, studious life. Within two months, she had dropped out of school, moved into a commune, and had a brush with the Moonies. She was chanting, praying, taking acid, and earning her living as a stripper. As always, when I heard what she was doing, I considered doing it myself. I was filled with envy at the thought of Nina's getting up on stage and being desired by all those men. Their lust I equated with an affirmation of her beauty.

When she came home to visit, she prayed to the Heavenly Father to protect her little sister. Then she showed me how to perform a striptease. Her dance was at once artistic and uninhibited, superbly coordinated and without rigid form. Her arms flailed, her back and torso undulated, her head swung as if disconnected from her body. Shaking with a rhythmic force, she maintained a firmly grounded stance, not so much dancing as allowing movement to pass through her. It was no ordinary striptease. Not once did she move her hips in the traditional bump and grind motion. Rather than peeling her clothes off in a slow and sinuous fashion, she fairly ripped them off. Her eyes looked inward with a fierce, almost angry expression. Her braided hair released itself into a mass of untamable curls; the unshaven black hair in her armpits and on her legs glistened. Pounding the floor with strong feet, punching the air with clenched fists, she was a tribal dancer performing a ritual dance of female sexuality.

Stripping, I believed, enabled her to portray herself so powerfully. My own little flirtations seemed feeble in comparison. If I were going to be as desirable as my sister, I decided, I was going to have to become a stripper. The motivation behind this decision was not one of simple, positive admiration. I wanted to dethrone Nina. My coronation would be her defeat.

Intoxicated with rivalry, I began to act very quickly. I gave little thought to my actions. I was mostly aware of a feeling in my gut, a feeling that I was not good enough, that I had to do something extraordinary to compete with my sister for the recognition of my beauty and, therefore, my worth. I felt a sense of immediacy, a need for haste, as if the prize that I was after were so elusive that it might vanish unless I pursued it at once. I did not think of practical things like the fact that I was in high school and did not have the time to work a stripper's six- or seven-day week. I did not think of the fact that I was only sixteen years old, and that I would be working illegally. I had a false identification card printed up in Nina's name in a shop I had seen many times on my way to work for Horace. I did not worry about explaining my whereabouts to any adults; no one monitored my comings and goings.

In a dim way, I feared my own momentum. I knew that I was moving too fast into a situation about which I knew nothing. I announced to several of my teachers that I was about to embark on a career in the Combat Zone. On some level, I wanted someone to stop me. No one did. I answered an ad in the newspaper that read, "Gogo Dancers Wanted. Top Pay." The agent urged me to come downtown to his office.

TWO

GOOD, CLEAN MONEY

"Can I help you, dear?" the man at the desk asked.

"I called earlier," I said, trying to sound nonchalant.

"You the girl who wants to model?"

"No, strip."

"Strip!" He jumped out of his chair, waving his arms in the air. With his greased hair and gold neck chains he looked like an extra from *West Side Story.* "We don't say strip. Never, never. Exotic dancing is an art. Anybody can take their clothes off, but how many people can do it with class? You need some sex appeal, a little charm, a hint of a smile." He flashed a white smile at me. "So call it dancing, sweetheart."

"Dancing," I corrected myself. "Do you have any openings?"

"Do we have any openings, she says. That's sweet. Listen, babe, exotic dancers are the only performers getting steady work in this town, and they make good, clean money. We have schoolteachers in this business and nurses and college girls. We even have girls coming in here who aren't old enough to work in the business. We weed them out." He looked closely at me. "How old are you?"

"Eighteen."

"Got an ID?" I handed it to him. He looked it over, tapped it, and tried to pull it apart. "You look young. But it says right here: Nina Lewin, eighteen years old. You sure this ain't your sister's?"

"It's mine," I assured him.

"You want work?" he asked. "Okay, if you look as good in the raw as you do right now, we'll put you to work."

He led me into his studio, a brightly lit room filled with camera equipment and paneled with photographs. The women in the pictures didn't have the thin sexiness I'd always strived for. More like the old-fashioned dames and gals of the movies, they had "cleavage" and "well-turned ankles." Beside them on the walls were similarly dated men, heavy-lidded lotharios with pencil-thin mustaches. One of them looked familiar.

"That's me," the agent said, "a few years back."

"You're an actor?"

"B. B. Jewel's the name. Actor, singer, comedian. Seemed like in 1974 nobody was working, except exotic dancers. So I retired as a performer and became an exotic agent." He flexed his muscles and winked at me. My face must not have registered comprehension, because he said, "That was a joke. You're supposed to laugh. How come you look so serious? You a runaway?"

"No." I forced a bit of a smile. I'd been trying to appear businesslike, thinking that made me seem older.

"That's better. Now, what name are you going to dance under?"

"Lolita."

"Spanish, eh? Are you going to do a little Spanish spitfire routine? Tell you the truth, I think you'd be better off with a French act. You buy your own props; I sell them cheap. Goes like this. You're coming home from a date, feeling good. You brush out your hair, take off all your clothes, jump into a bathtub, come out of the bathtub, wipe yourself, powder yourself, and jump into bed."

"I have to do all that? I thought I'd just dance."

"You can jazz it up if you want to, but all you got to do is take off one piece of clothing at a time. You do end up completely naked on the stage, not a stitch left on. Keep an open mind on it. You're not going to have to lay down on the floor and have the gynecologists all hanging around you. There's no big spreads, no fornication, no audience participation. All you're doing is dancing, three, four, five twenty-minute sets a day."

"What's the salary?"

"Salary, she says. Honey, we're not getting you a basketball contract. You get paid by the shift. How much? Well, that depends on your qualifications, which I haven't seen yet." He strode to the doorway and stood there, with his toes at the line of the entrance. "Where are my feet?"

"Your feet? In the doorway, I suppose."

"Good. And they're going to stay here. I won't go one step further until you put your clothes back on. Now, I want you to take everything off and turn around once."

Should I run now, I wondered, before I ended up naked and alone with a man I didn't know? He could rape me and no one would believe me. What were you doing in his office with your clothes off? they'd say. What did you expect? I thought I'd audition in a bar, where the lights were low. There, I'd be one of many women, my own nudity buffered by theirs. Here I'd be inspected, a lone specimen under high wattage.

"I think I'll wait to see if I like any of the bars," I said.

"You think you're going to pick and choose? I'll send you to the best club in Boston, but I've got to know what I'm sending them. It's no big deal. Just lift your dress up and slip

29

out of your panties. I've seen more on a beach. Girls let their bikinis fall off all the time, and they don't get paid for it, either."

That's true, I thought. I'd undressed with men I hardly knew, many times. I always ran the risk of rape. Nakedness was natural, the primal costume. What could be more beautiful than a woman's body, unadorned? As B. B. Jewel said, exotic dancing was an art, a clean art. Besides, Nina did it; she must have had to undress in front of an agent.

"Look, honey, Lolita," he implored. "A good-looking girl with a nice body should make a lot of money. That doesn't mean anybody has to touch you. Even if you're shook out of your shoes, you should give it a try. You might like it. If you don't, we'll say thank you and forget it. This is 1976. You're not doing anything against the law, you're not doing anything against your will, and you'll be the one laughing all the way to the bank every week. It doesn't make you dirty. If you're a virgin right now, you'll stay a virgin."

In my room all week, I'd practiced stripping in front of the mirror. I'd watched myself attempt the most alluring poses, imagining that a rapt audience sat just beyond my view. I'd felt no fear, only a vague sense of excitement, a romantic longing for the flowers and applause that would surely follow my act. If I'd already envisioned stripping for one hundred men, why stall in front of one?

With shaking hands, I quickly pulled off my clothes, spun around, and began to dress again.

"Hold it a minute!" B. B. Jewel yelled, breaking his promise not to step beyond the doorway. "I need to take your measurements. What's the rush? You got to be someplace?"

"I guess I'm kind of nervous." I continued to dress.

"Everybody is at first. Who wouldn't be, unless she's already been a hooker? And I'll give any girl a chance, as long as she abides by my rules: Be to work on time, call if you can't make it, don't bring boyfriends in the club, and don't go out with

30

customers or other employees, male or female. If a girl comes in off the street, she's asking for a chance. Once she starts making money for herself or her kid, not for a pimp, she'll never want to hook again." Before I could object, he took my measurements. Then he recorded them on a note card, snapped a Polaroid picture of me and taped that to the card as well. "This way I know who I'm talking to when you call up. Lo-lee-ta. About as tough as a kitten, and I broke you in myself. Wasn't so bad, was it? You've already done the hardest thing."

"What are my hours?" I asked.

"You still need to audition. I'll take you down to the Twilight Lounge. Harry'll love you. Eighteen, you say? You're a doll."

B. B. Jewel led me through a busy intersection in downtown Boston. As we crossed the street, the surroundings suddenly changed. We walked by no more office buildings with cavernous lobbies and uniformed doormen. Instead, we passed dimly lit entrances to bars with names like the Sweetheart Lounge, the Showtime Cabaret, and the Kittykat Klub. Posted outside the bars were pictures of women who supposedly worked inside. They posed in skimpy outfits. In one picture, a woman lay on her side, propped up on her arm; her other arm was tucked between her tight-closed bare legs. She was winking. The caption under another woman's picture said, "Sandy. 42-24-36." Her chest was thrust forward, her back was swayed, and her smile said, Get any closer and I'll belt you one. I wanted to stop to look at these women, to try to learn something from their poses and expressions about what I was about to walk into. I felt less and less brave as we walked deeper into the Combat Zone. I could smell stale beer and hear the refrains of popular disco songs as we walked by the bars. I felt heady and unsure of myself.

The physical reality of the Zone put a knife into my fantasies. My image of the strip joint had been a fantastic conglomeration of several myths. I'd imagined the Folies Bergère, with

31

its feathery costumes and marble staircases. I'd imagined shimmying, sultry-eyed harem girls beneath their sultan's canopy. I'd imagined wood nymphs dancing lithely across woods and streams. I'd never imagined a dark bar jammed into a city block alongside greasy pizza counters, "adult" bookstores, and overflowing garbage cans.

My gut reaction was that what I saw was wrong; it simply should not be. I considered ways to tell the agent that I had changed my mind and didn't want to strip after all. I felt that I had committed myself, and that I could not leave like a child, on a whim. And so I followed B. B. Jewel into a bar that I mistrusted even from the outside.

What remains with me from my first day at the Twilight Lounge is a collage of faces, conversations, and impressions. I cannot remember the sequence of events. I remember fragments.

The spotlight and many pairs of eyes focused on a tall, black-haired woman who knelt on the stage. She wore a leopard suit and she barely moved. She gnashed her teeth and twirled her leopard tail menacingly at the audience. Her name was Revenge. She fondled a penis-shaped plastic banana; her fingers ran up and down its shaft.

A rickety spiral staircase led up to a dressing room paneled with mirrors. I saw a dozen reflections of myself, on the walls, the ceiling, the tables, a dozen small, pale young women dressed in street clothes and trying not to stare at the parade of female bodies in various stages of semi-attire. There were women my mother's age and women my age, women of many races and nationalities. I tried not to stare at their breasts. Some were tiny pubescent nubs, some were hanging and often-nursed, some were hard silicone lumps sheathed by sagging, jaundiced skin. There were smooth, muscular thighs and thighs dimpled with fat. One woman was underweight, her skin like a dangerously thin layer of ice over a diseased interior. Another

32

woman's belly cascaded from the confines of a tight bodice.

I had thought of the stripper as the woman who possessed a consummate sexual magnetism. Each of these women must have embodied that perfection. They were not replicas of Miss America, and yet they dared to show their bodies in public. My standards for judging relative beauty were no longer adequate. For the first time since I was a little child, I did not want to, and I could not, assign each woman her proper slot in an arbitrary hierarchy of beauty. I looked, I stared, and for the first time I saw what women's bodies looked like: the curves, angles, creases, and folds. With so much variety, and none like the blue-light projections on my TV screen, how could I pass judgment?

Two women talked to each other through the mirror while studying their own reflections. "I'm out of here in a month," said one.

"You've been saying that for a year."

"Yeah, well I've got a straight job lined up. Decent pay, no hassles. I'm getting out. You get old fast around here."

"I know it. My legs look like an old lady's, veins popping through all over. I'm getting out, too. My man's gonna work. I'll be sitting home painting my nails."

"That lazy sonuvabitch never worked a day in his life. You'll be here as long as you keep him around."

Also reflected in the mirrors were glittering rhinestones and sequins, phosphorescent little pots and tubes of stage makeup, long chiffon gowns draped over chairs, ashtrays filled to the brim with cigarette butts and unfinished joints, bar glasses half full with melting ice, and discarded hypodermic needles. A blond wig rested on a mannequin's head, the artificial scalp beginning to show beneath a balding patch. A poster in one corner showed a naked woman sitting with her legs wide open, smiling serenely.

In the corner, two women hunched protectively over a hand

mirror. One of them poured white powder from a tiny glass vial onto the mirror and slashed the powder with a razor blade.

"This is some good blow," she said. "Never been cut."

"Let the new girl try it," someone suggested.

"What is it?" I wanted to know.

"Just try some, baby."

She thrust the mirror under my nose and handed me a silver straw. I sniffed hard, drawing the powder up through my nostril into the back of my throat. Almost immediately a pleasant sensation swept over me.

"Do the other line," she demanded.

I finished what was left on the mirror.

"That's twenty, when you get paid."

Everyone laughed.

Out in the bar, the costumes dazed me. There were long gowns of every color, ornamented with beads, feathers, sequins, and rhinestones. One dancer wore the ceremonial dress of an Indian princess. Her skirt, made of soft leather, and bordered with highly intricate, brightly colored beadwork, lapped about the tops of her high-heeled moccasins. Her headpiece rose two feet above her, and trailed down to the floor, a rush of blue feathers on white velvet. Another dancer was disguised as a conquistadora. She whirled out of billowing layers of red to reveal three more layers of costume. The first was a tight bodice of black leather. The second was red and lacy. The third was a barely visible armor, a thin silver chain that fit around her fingers, crawled up her arms, draped over her shoulders, outlined her breasts, encircled her thighs, ran up her back, and clasped around her neck.

My audition took place on a makeshift stage in an empty room behind the main barroom. Harry Chester, the boss, was summoned for the occasion. He lumbered into the room chomping on a cigar and rubbing his inflated belly. He brought with him an assistant, an older woman with a blond beehive hairdo.

34

"Let's see it," he demanded.

"Do you want me to take my clothes off and turn around once?" I asked.

"I want you to do your routine, like you'd do on stage."

"I don't have a routine. B. B. Jewel said they'd train me on the job, if I had the qualifications."

Chester laughed. "I don't know what you got till you cut the crap and take it off."

"You're scaring the dickens out of her, Harry," the assistant said. "Honey, it's easy. You like to dance? Hear the music? Well, dance to it. Act a little sexy and take off one piece of your costume at a time."

For a costume I'd been given a faded red negligee, a black bra that snapped in the front, and a dingy triangle of black satin called a G-string. On my feet, I wore a pair of gold spike-heeled pumps, a size too large. Act sexy? Did that mean batting my eyelashes, grinding my hips, or coming up with a gimmick like Revenge's plastic squirting banana? I faintly remembered a cartoon portrayal of the prototypical seductress in black who lifted her eyebrows three times, leaned backward with her hands on her hips, and took long slow steps toward our unsuspecting hero, the victim of her lust. For lack of any other idea of what to do, I decided to try that.

Chester doubled over in laughter. "Where'd she get that? Oh, my God! Save my heart!"

That must not be right. I wanted him to be awed into silent wonder at the power of my sexuality, not to laugh. Maybe I should tempt him a bit before I let him see my "qualifications." Looking him straight in the eye, I pulled down the shoulder strap of my negligee, then pulled it back up, repeating this motion perhaps ten times.

"This is great!" he howled. "Precious. Where'd B.B. find her? Lolita, I'm going to make you a star."

"Cut it out, Harry," the assistant said. "Take off the negligee, honey. That's right, lift it over your head."

What next? Should I take off my bra and G-string and get it over with? No, this was a strip*tease*. I'd tease; but how? All I could think of doing was unsnapping my bra and flapping it open and closed, offering peeks of my breasts.

"She thinks she's a penguin," was Chester's comment. "I ain't got all day, babe. Take it off, would you?"

I took off the G-string and stepped out of my shoes, thinking they wanted me totally nude. Again, Chester roared, "The shoes stay on! Your legs need the extra length. Candy, see that she gets some new shoes. We'll start you this afternoon, Lolita. Don't ask me why. That's the best laugh I've had since the girl from Las Vegas almost got choked by her snake."

"Don't mind him," Candy soothed me as Chester left. "He does that to all the new girls. Wants to see how tough they are. We'll get you a costume and take it out of your pay. You can watch today. Tomorrow we'll put you on stage with another girl, to get you used to it."

"I'm going to need a while to get used to it."

"Are you action?" she asked.

"Action? I guess so."

"Lesson number one," she said. "Don't say yes to anything unless you know what it means. What I'm asking is, How much are you going to charge a guy for a good time?"

"I've never charged a guy for a good time."

She rolled her eyes. "Maybe Harry's right about you. Well, you'll learn quick enough."

Between my shows, Candy explained, I must convince the customers to buy drinks for me. A dancer's drink cost six dollars. If I met my daily quota of twelve drinks, I'd get one dollar for each drink I sold. If I didn't, I wouldn't get any commission. The bartenders tallied the drinks on a sheet of paper, putting a check by the dancer's name for each sale she made.

"Won't I get drunk?"

"There's no alcohol in the drinks, unless you say, Make it strong. That's why we call it hustling. You're putting something over on them."

"Why would a guy spend six dollars for a drink?"

"He doesn't pay to get in here. And you can make him think you're worth it. Promise anything. Usually, you don't take him out back unless he buys champagne, fifty, seventy-five, or one hundred dollar bottles. You get the bottle in a bucket, with half of it already dumped out. When you fill your glass up, keep on pouring over the rim. The booze'll go into the bucket, and the guy'll never know. You end up drinking about a glassful. Anything else you do in the back room is your business. If you don't do right by a guy, he won't ask for you again. Of course, we'd like you to make the customer happy. We'll have to let you go if you can't please any of them."

She told me that I'd be paid in cash every Sunday. They'd start me at forty dollars a day and raise it to fifty dollars after a few weeks, if I did the job well. I'd work six days a week.

Lowering her voice, she said, "You can double that in tips. Just don't name a price before you deliver. It's hard to tell a cop from a john."

"It's illegal?"

"Sure it's illegal. Illegal for the club, not the girl. Don't worry about it, honey. Watch the other girls, and you'll do fine."

That afternoon, I sat at the bar watching the nonstop succession of performers. At one point, another dancer sat beside me. She deliberately overturned a glassful of small drinking straws and began to order them into piles. Then she scrambled the straws and rearranged them into five smaller heaps. She seemed determined to find the correct pattern.

After watching her reshuffle the straws a few times, I asked, "What are you doing?"

"Counting the days till Charlie comes."

"Who's Charlie?"

"My old man. He won't leave me here much longer. Twenty-seven days."

"Then where are you going?"

"Oh, I don't know, exactly." She reached up to smooth back her hair. Missing her head by several inches, she stroked the air instead; she didn't seem to notice. "We're getting married. Charlie's gonna work for my dad, in the store, and we're getting a kitten, one of those little Siamese ones that goes 'Waaaa,' real loud. 'Waaaa,' like a baby." She leaned over the bar, laughing, and messed up her neat rows of straws. I'd never seen anyone so drunk, and I stared at her. "Why're you looking at me like that? What's your name?"

"Lolita."

"I'm Charlene." Slowly, trying to balance herself, she stood up. "I got to go sit with my regular now. How about, after work, we go get a drink some place outside of the Zone? I'm supposed to meet this guy, but we can go out the back door; he'll wait awhile and then go home. You want to? I'll buy."

"Okay," I agreed.

At eight o'clock, Charlene came looking for me, drunker than before. She left work wearing all of her makeup and an outfit that could have been a costume, for all it covered. She loomed almost a foot above me in her heels. We walked as quickly as she could walk through the thickening crowd of men in the Zone. In the dark, the district possessed more of the character I'd imagined. Neon lights flashed the names of star performers; tuxedoed doormen stood outside the clubs urging men to come inside.

"Looking good," a man in a hat called after us.

"Pimp," Charlene identified him. "Thinks he's cool."

She took me to a bar in a hotel at the far edge of the Zone. When the bouncer there refused to accept my identification card, we decided to go for coffee instead.

In the light of the coffee shop, I could see Charlene clearly for the first time. She wore her blond hair in a sophisticated French twist around her head. On her finger she wore a small diamond ring. Her hands were small and never still. They reached to pat her hair, to straighten her dress, to gesture. Always, they stopped before completing an action, as if magnetically repelled from contact with anything. The lines on her face, I could see, were the marks of stress and lack of sleep; she was hardly older than I was.

During the two hours we sat drinking coffee, she became lucid at times, incoherent at others. I listened to her in fascination.

"If my daddy didn't leave, I wouldn't be messed up in all this." She gestured widely. "I'd still be in New Jersey."

"Doing what?"

"I don't know. Hairdressing school. Daddy said no to that. He said I was smart enough to be a doctor, but I'd never make it through eight years of school without getting married. So I could be a nurse, except nurses have to take orders from doctors. If I was smart, I'd marry a doctor. That's what he said before he left, two weeks before I turned sixteen."

"Why'd he leave?"

"I don't know. He loved me. I started going with boys after he left, and he called me one day. Said, 'Boys don't like to kiss girls who blow.' He cares about me. I know he does. He always said I was his prettiest girl."

"You are pretty," I said. A few tears had carried streaks of mascara down an otherwise flawless face.

"My mother used to dress me up. She was fat. Now she's dead. She dressed me for my junior high prom. I looked like Miss Budding Barbie doll, and those boys wouldn't dance with me. After, she took me down to the diner. All the sailors were whistling and waving at me. I never felt so ashamed."

When I asked her how she'd started stripping, she launched into a long story.

At the age of sixteen, she'd gone with her friend Terri to a basketball game in New York City. After the game, a man in a big red hat approached the girls. "Did you like the game?" he asked. "Number 44 is my cousin. Would you like to meet him?"

"Wow! Yeah, I want to go get his autograph," Charlene said.

Terri, who was from the city, hissed, "No! Don't you go near him. Can't you tell from looking at him he's a pimp?"

Charlene didn't know what a pimp was. She just wanted to meet Number 44. So she went with this man, whom she called Red Hat, to his car. He convinced her that she could make some easy fast money by handing someone a handkerchief filled with cocaine, and drove her off to a building near Times Square.

He took her into a room furnished only with an unmade bed. There, he broke out the cocaine, and said, "Do some."

"No," she said, "I don't like it."

"DO IT!"

Frightened, then, that he'd hurt her, she did it. "When are we going to meet your cousin?" she asked.

"Got to wait for the dude to pick us up," he said. "And don't sit on that bed. Make it." Well trained by her mother in obedience and housekeeping, she made the bed. He brought her into another room for a few minutes; when they returned to the original room, the bed was unmade. "Make it," he demanded again. He went to the window and shouted down, "No, you can't come up here yet."

"Come on," she heard a woman cry, "it's cold down here."

Red Hat took Charlene into a bathroom. "Take off your pants," he ordered. She refused. "TAKE THEM OFF!" He yanked them down and began to beat her. Then he raped her. When he was done, he took her into the other room, where the woman from the street waited.

"Charlene's going to be living with us," he said.

Still denying what was happening to her, Charlene said,

40

"No, I'm not. We're just going to sell this coke and go meet Number 44." She spent the night in a bed with Red Hat and the other woman.

In the morning, she discovered that he had stolen her ID from her pocketbook. He said, "I want you to stay here and work for me. If you don't, I'm going to go back and tell your family, your friends, everyone, that you are a prostitute." Imagining that her father would find out and lose respect for her, and too frightened to realize that no one would believe this pimp, she agreed to it. She spent a week out on the street turning tricks with the other woman, who "loved Red Hat and wanted to marry him."

At the end of the week, the police picked her up. They'd seen the mimeographed pictures her mother had passed out to all the precincts. Feeling guilty, as if she'd brought the events on herself by being too pretty, too provocative, she refused to press charges.

Meanwhile, her friend Terri envied Charlene's adventure. Terri searched out Red Hat, went to Boston with him, and began working for him. When he got shot and paralyzed, Terri found another pimp. Charlene began to go up to Boston and tag along with Terri to the bars. After her abduction, she felt that she'd hit rock bottom; nothing could shock her. She didn't want to turn tricks, but she enjoyed playing the role of the prostitute: dressing like one, acting like one. Among pimps and hookers, no one accused her of being too sexy.

Then Terri got a job at the Twilight Lounge. Harry Chester would ask Charlene, "When are you coming to work for me?"

She'd say, "No, no. I'm going to finish high school."

As soon as she finished high school, she came to work for Chester. She'd been there for three months now. She planned to leave soon, because she'd met a guy named Charlie in New Jersey. He adored her. As soon as he could afford it, he'd come get her. He'd given her a diamond engagement ring.

"And Charlie'll work for my dad," Charlene told me. "I heard Daddy's got a store now."

"That'll be good," I said, exhausted. I'd become so involved in her story that I wanted to go down to New Jersey and bring Charlie back myself.

Working at Horace's, I had met many men with rough stories to tell, but I had never met a woman like Charlene before that night. When we parted, I watched her, still drunk, walking back toward the Zone to catch a cab.

On the subway back to Brookline, I began to write down everything I'd seen and heard that day. Each word, each sight, each person I'd encountered made me feel a little bit more mature. I didn't want to be one more kid from Brookline High School whose life ambition was to go to a fancy college. Now I'd seen the real world.

In the mornings I went to high school and in the afternoons I worked in the Twilight Lounge. During my first week at the club, I watched other dancers interact with the customers. I watched a woman named Mercedes come down into the audience after finishing her act, wearing nothing but a bra and a G-string. She would sidle up to a customer, put her tongue in his ear, her hand on his groin, and ask him if he would like some company. Her approach was effective; men bought many drinks for her. Dancers whispered promises of the gifts they would impart if a man would buy them a bottle of champagne. "Buy me a one-hundred-dollar bottle and I'll knock your socks off." "We'll have a party, just you and me." In the back room, women fulfilled their promises. They gave hand-jobs and blow-jobs. Some of them sat on the customers' laps and had sexual intercourse with them right there in the booths. Cookie would let men crawl under the table and have oral sex with her; for that she charged fifty dollars. I learned to try to have the least amount of sexual contact for the most money, to try to put off the inevitable sexual encounter until the man had bought at least two bottles of champagne, and then to follow through only if the man insisted. Finally, with no illusions of romance, I learned to get the dirty business done as quickly as possible.

For a week I did this. I paraded around the bar in three little triangles of satin that barely covered my breasts and pubic hair. I let men squeeze my ass while they decided whether they would buy me a drink. I told the most foul-breathed old men that they were good-looking. I promised to make them feel "real good" if they bought me champagne. With the champagne in hand, I led them to the back room, where I caressed and fondled them with my hands and lips. I allowed them to poke their fingers into my body. Sometimes I had the courage to ask them for a ten dollar tip, and sometimes I didn't. I thought that the back room was one of the duties of the job, that I was expected to render these services for my daily wage of forty dollars.

For a week I left the club feeling soiled. I felt the imprint of anonymous hands on my body and tasted the sour tobacco of many men's saliva in my mouth. I thought of my sore vagina as the tomb for their intrusive probes. I went home and showered until my skin cried for mercy, and still I felt dirty. I douched, gargled, scrubbed, and soaked until the only part of me that was not antiseptic was my memory.

I wanted to learn about the Combat Zone, a world that was foreign and unfathomable to me, but I did not want it to touch me. It was exciting to be admired by hundreds of men; I didn't want to feel the ultimate impact of their admiration. I wanted their attention, not their sweat and semen. I began to think about what a dancer named Brandy had told me: "You've got to have a gimmick." She did not mind giving hand-jobs; when men asked her to do anything else, she told them she had V.D. Charlene's gimmick was that men could touch her but she would not touch them. Robin touched the men but would not let them touch her. A gimmick was a way of setting limits to what one would do, without angering or disappointing the customer. If I were going to survive at the job, I needed a gimmick that would enable me to convince men to buy me champagne, elude all of their advances, and leave them feeling satisfied.

The next day a man bought me a one-hundred-dollar bottle of champagne. I promised him that we'd have a good time, nothing more explicit. We sat in a booth in the back room. In the far corner I saw a dancer with another customer. I could make out only their shadows: her body curved over his, her head in his lap. With his hand on my shoulder, my customer pulled me closer to him. He said, "Get me off now. Do something for me."

I said, "You know the Lord Jesus Christ is your savior."

He jerked his hand from my shoulder as if he'd been burned by the first sparks from hell. "What was that now?"

"Aren't you a Christian?"

"Yeah, I'm a Christian. What does that have to do with anything?"

"I am here in this house of corruption to spread the word of the Lord. I pose as a stripper, but I am like Mary Magdalene. I have seen my Lord and I have reformed. Jesus forgave me, and he will forgive you, too, if you will pray."

"Listen, Lolita, I'm Catholic, and I go to church and all, but I really had something kind of different in mind."

"Do you know that Jesus loves you?"

"Yeah, I know, I know. Oh, Jesus! I come to the Combat Zone looking for a little relief and I get this. A hundred bucks down the drain!"

"Amen. Whatever you give to Jesus will come right back to you. Do you know how lucky you are that you gave your money to a holy cause? Do you know how close you came to sinning?"

We talked about why he hardly ever went to church, why he came to the Combat Zone, why he wanted to leave his wife after fifteen years of marriage. He bought me another bottle of champagne so that we could continue our conversation. When he left, he thanked me for offering him redemption instead of a hand-job. He paid me what was in his mind a compliment: "You've got a lot of balls."

I used this technique with similar results for two weeks. Not every man was thrilled to have spent his money for an afternoon in church when he wanted sex, but every man took his hands off me. Sometimes customers left quickly, aware that I was not going to bend. Most, however, wanted to talk about their relationship with God or the Church. Whereas an appeal to a man's sensitivity or empathy with me as a human being, or as a worker, would not have been effective, an appeal to his Christian upbringing, which was replete with guilt and fear of being caught in acts of sin by the ever-watching eye of God, worked without fail. A woman who would not have sex for money, enough money (every woman has a price), was not part of their reality; a missionary devoted to saving souls was believable to them. I, in turn, was able to escape, at least superficially, feeling contaminated.

One man did not accept my gimmick. He was a huge potbellied man who spoke a language of monosyllabic grunts. After he succumbed to my promises that it would be worth his while to spend one hundred dollars on a bottle of champagne, we went to the back room. No one else was back there at the time. He put his arm around me; I removed it.

He said, "Do something for me."

I said, "You know the Lord Jesus Christ is your savior."

"Suck me off."

"I'm here to spread the word of the Lord."

"I go to church for that. Now get me off, you little bitch."

"I'm like Mary Magdalene."

He reached down toward his belt. So, I thought, he's going to show me his penis, as if that will change my mind. I prepared to feign indignant innocence. But I heard a faint click, then saw the flash of a blade as it flipped out of its sheath. I froze; my terror crystallized on the tip of his switchblade. *I'm going to die. I'm three years old. Mommy and Daddy are fighting;*

they're going to leave me. I'm going to die. I'm fourteen years old. The man grabs my breast and chases me down the street, breathing 'I'm not going to hurt you' down my neck. I'm going to die.

"Now you're going to do what I say." He grazed the knife against the side of my neck and nicked my skin. I did not sit and weigh my options, or think of ways to talk to him, or think of routes of escape. I did what he wanted. He grunted and left the bar quickly.

Crying, bleeding, spitting, and hysterical, I crashed into Harry Chester's office. He sat at his big desk, surrounded by photographs of his favorite strippers: beautiful Lilly with her boa constrictor, Killer Kelly with her forty-eight-inch bust. He chewed on a fat cigar. The three-hundred-pound bouncer stood at the door. "You filthy scum," I shouted. "You don't protect your girls. Look what happened to me. Look at me!" He looked up, unalarmed, and blew smoke in my face. "I quit!" I shrieked. "You pig." I had been working for this man for three weeks. He had summoned me to his office several times to tell me that I had the makings of a star, if I would invest money in costumes. After the first week, he told me that payday was every other Sunday. After the second week, he said that payday came every third Sunday. Out of the "goodness of his heart" he had lent me fifty dollars of the seven hundred he owed me. "Who are you?" He looked me in the eye as he asked it. "I've never seen you before. Get out of here. I don't ever want to see your face again." He motioned to the bouncer. I knew that I was powerless, and I left.

THREE

THIS IS SHOW BUSINESS

As I left the Twilight Lounge with no pay for three weeks' work, I felt angry and I felt powerless to avenge my anger. This enraged impotence mingled with a sense of shame and guilt that I had ultimately given in to the man's desires. My feelings of powerlessness shocked me into a reminder that I was not Lolita or Mary Magdalene. I was a sixteen-year-old high school student working illegally at a job that I believed was controlled by organized crime. I had walked blindly into a situation where no one could afford to be naïve. As I saw it, my attacker and my innocence were the culprits, the cause of my pain. Stripping itself was not intrinsically evil; it had to be approached properly.

For the next year, I went back to high school. No longer dividing my time between the Combat Zone and the classroom, I devoted all of my time to my schoolwork. Then, shortly after turning eighteen, I entered college to study psychology. Although my father sent money, he never sent enough. I supported myself by working as a waitress, a temporary office worker, and a salad preparer in a restaurant. I disliked all these jobs, and I resented doing dull, often strenuous, work for minimum wage. Although I knew that Nina had quit her job and that I'd be alone in the venture this time, I decided to try stripping again.

The Combat Zone had been in the news that year. A Harvard football player had been stabbed in a fight there; he'd died shortly thereafter. The Zone had been put on trial. Police had appeared on the streets and the vice squad had set out to squelch prostitution.

I could sense a difference as I walked down Washington Street. Some of the clubs appeared to be complying with the police regulations. The idea of legitimacy had become their sales pitch. As a mascot, they offered the smiling, blond-haired, eighteen-year-old girl who danced, not because Welfare had cut her check in half and her kids were hungry, but because she loved to take her clothes off for men she didn't know. The Zone was going to be a place where college boys could come for a fun, harmless night out. Some of the clubs advertised an "All-Nude College Girl Revue."

Located three doors down from the Twilight Lounge, the Nudie-Tease Nightclub was such a bar. In its tasteful window displays, pasties covered the women's nipples. The dancers' expressions in these photographs looked playful rather than seductive.

"I'm so sorry to hear about your experiences at the Twilight Lounge," said Preston Cara, the owner of the Nudie-Tease. "My name stands for fairness in the Zone. My girls are paid every Tuesday, and we have no quota on drinks."

"I don't have to hustle?"

"We say 'mixing,' not hustling. We charge seven dollars for dancers' drinks; you get a buck twenty-five cut. I couldn't afford to run the place otherwise. However, I will not tolerate any prostitution whatsoever on the premises."

Young and well spoken, Preston told me that he wanted "his

48

girls" to get along with each other. Job advancement would come rapidly to an intelligent and motivated girl like me, he said. He auditioned me and hired me to work four days a week. "And do something about that hair," he added. "You look like a Brillo lightbulb on stage."

The next day, I carried my motley collection of costumes to the dressing room. I hadn't stayed at my previous job long enough to collect a fancy wardrobe. I'd usually stripped out of the velvet gowns I'd saved from my job at Horace's. My dresses were elegant but out of date, antiques salvaged from the attics of charitable old ladies. I'd even pilfered a pair of lacy gloves from my grandmother; if she noticed, I planned to explain to her that they were the latest fashion in Boston.

At first I thought the dressing room was empty. Then I heard a rumbling in the corner. When I looked, I saw a woman leaning into her locker, taking a swig of whiskey.

"Is that you, Rebel?" she whined.

"No, it's Lolita. I'm new here."

"Lolita," the voice said. "I've heard that name before. They made a movie about you and your daddy. He really loved you, didn't he? I wish I had a daddy like that."

I knew the voice. It sounded flat, drunk, and familiar. The woman's back was to me; I could see that she was tall and that she wore her blond hair wrapped around her head. She flasked her whiskey, then tried to stand up. Making a vague attempt to straighten her hair, her hands stopped in mid-gesture.

"Charlene?"

She turned around, surprised. "Do I know you?"

"Don't you remember, at the Twilight Lounge, we went out for coffee one night?"

"Yeah, I worked there. They fired me. I don't know why. Something about I fell asleep and this guy bought me champagne and I wasn't doing anything for him. I don't know."

"This club is better?"

"Sure, it's better. I guess."

"Didn't Charlie ever show up?" I asked. In my mind, Charlene had been married and settled for over a year.

Her lips began to shake. I didn't know if she would cry or smile. She smiled, and the creeping red capillaries around her nose, the sign of too much drink over a long period of time, spread out across her face. "Of course he came. Charlie, he came. He's good to me, too."

"Did you get married?"

"We're getting married. Charlie needs a job first. He can do lots of things, especially sales. He just needs to find the right job for him. That can take a while, you know."

"He doesn't mind your stripping?"

"He wants me to do it, for a time now. We need the money. He said I can quit soon, and then we'll get married. We're gonna have a baby."

"You're pregnant?"

"No, but Charlie says I'll make a good mother."

I envied her. My love life consisted of a series of affairs, none lasting longer than a few months. Always alert for the man who would love me unconditionally, I had not yet found him. Because being manless struck me as being armless, homeless, lifeless, I went to bed with dozens of men, hoping each time that I'd found my future husband. I pictured my ideal man as dark-haired, tall, and poetic. We would read Shakespeare together and appreciate each other's brilliant interpretations of difficult passages. He'd be somewhat older than I, and would help me mold whatever raw intelligence I had into incisive perceptions. We'd make love often and with intense passion. Although he'd think I was beautiful and praise me excessively, he wouldn't love me because he found me beautiful. And that's where my fantasy got snagged. How would we get to know each other if not through sex? How could I keep a man's interest long enough to convince him of my worth unless I slept with him?

One of my first lovers had taught me an important lesson. We had just made love, and we lay in bed caressing each other. He pointed to my vagina and said, "It's tired."

"It?" I asked. "You mean me?"

"No, I mean it."

At first I felt disturbed by his insistence that my genitals, not I, had been active and passionately involved. A few days later, as I sat by the telephone waiting for his call, which never came, I began to wish that I could separate my techniques and body and sexuality from my sense of self. My vagina felt sensations, not emotions, and could not be hurt in the same way I could. Being female meant waiting by the phone for his call; if I called him, he'd consider me overly aggressive and not want to see me, anyway. If I could get the sex I wanted without feeling so raw and open, I'd be better off. So I tried to sever the connection between my feelings and my body. I'd actively seek out the sex I desired and then passively experience it, experience it as if it were happening to some other person who just happened to be located between my legs. I felt all the sensations of pleasure, but I did not connect them to any need for love.

At the same time, I wanted to be looked upon and admired by men. In the absence of such attention, I began to feel that I had no hope, even, of getting what I wanted. The more a man adored my body, the more likely he'd want to continue to see me. My body became the bait with which to lure a man, unknowing, into loving me.

Shortly before I went to work at the Nudie-Tease, I met a man named Jack. True to my pattern, I went to bed with him soon after I met him. He was an artist, and he asked me to pose for him. Every afternoon for several weeks, we went to his studio, where I lay nude as he tried to capture me in charcoal. I enjoyed having him study my body. "You're beautiful," he'd say, "like a little doll." Yet the drawings looked nothing like me. Attributing the dissimilarity to his lack of skill as an artist, I continued to see him. We talked very little, but we made love

51

wonderfully. Each night as he left my house, I wondered if, finally, through my body, I'd found a man who could love me. After several weeks, I grew impatient with his nightly departures; I wanted to spend the whole night together. Then the truth came out. He lived with a woman and wanted a casual affair. I stopped seeing him.

I felt angry with myself for letting my expectations run so high. It made no sense to give my body to someone who didn't particularly care about me unless I got something in return. What did I get from Jack? Attention. I could get the same attention from the men in a strip joint, and get paid for it, as well. Besides, in a strip joint, the boundaries were clear. I could get nothing but attention from the men there. I knew they wouldn't love me. Perhaps if I got attention at work, I'd be freer to find love outside of work. Lolita could deal with one set of needs, Lauri with another.

A loud knock at the dressing-room door jolted me out of my thoughts that first day at the Nudie-Tease.

"Come on in," Charlene called out.

A middle-aged woman entered the dressing room, pulling a large suitcase.

"Oh, no!" Charlene gasped. "I don't have your money. See, Charlie, he needed a new shirt."

"I don't know who Charlie is," the woman said. "Don't worry, I got my money. B. B. Jewel took it out of your pay. See why it helps to have an agent? You got one?" she asked me.

"No, he didn't help me too much the first time around."

"She's smart," the woman said.

We introduced ourselves. Her name was Desiree. She'd been a career stripper for about twenty-five years, until the only clubs that would hire her were places she wouldn't go. Rundown bars on rural routes, where she had to dance on tabletops or narrow strips of plywood, didn't suit her at all. She had seen burlesque in its heyday. Striptease still had an aura of legitimacy back then, when Gypsy Rose Lee traveled the carnival route, and Sally Rand stood naked behind stuffed swans and ostrich plumes. Desiree loved the life. She tried to prolong her stay in the business by getting silicone injections in her breasts and buttocks.

"That kept me going a few more years," she said. "When I turned forty-five, I knew I'd had it. So I went into the costume-making business, and I'm the best around. Isn't that so, Charlene."

"The best," Charlene agreed emphatically. "I have two Desirees, my blue one, and my southern belle costume, the white one."

"Show them to Lolita," Desiree urged her.

Charlene walked over to her locker, stole a quick slug of whiskey, and then brought out the most beautiful dress I had ever seen. She handled it gently, making sure that the sleeves didn't drag on the floor. Desiree took the dress and hung it on a hook in front of me. I stared at her intricate handiwork. It must have taken her hours to attach the rows of white beads to the borders of the dress. Drawn in at the waist and flouncing out dramatically at the hips, the dress looked like a relic from a southern plantation that had been recovered and redecorated by some very rich lady of the twentieth century. The fine white lace around the collar and cuffs contrasted with the brighter white sequins at the waistline.

"Put it on," Desiree ordered. "Let's give her the full effect."

Obediently, Charlene disrobed and stood very still as Desiree dressed her. Fully dressed, she looked splendid. Like a true "southern belle," she was completely white: her hair, her skin, her dress. The corset pushed her breasts up; they looked full and smooth, ready to burst through the fabric. She breathed shallowly, left with little room by the tight waistband. Her hips looked full and well protected.

"Isn't she gorgeous?" Desiree sighed. "I'm taking fifty dollars out of her pay each week. In five months she'll own it. Meanwhile, she gets to wear it."

"I don't wear it here," Charlene said. "I'm getting married in it."

Desiree shrugged her shoulders. "That's up to you what you do with it. I have to warn you, Rebel wants one, too. If you don't start wearing it, she's got every right to order one."

"Rebel's got fifty costumes, already," Charlene complained. "Why does she need what I've got?"

"Rebel's our up-and-coming little star, darling. Don't you know a rising star when you see one?"

"Preston told me he'd put my picture out front, as soon as I straighten up a little bit. He says I've got it over Rebel any day." Charlene's eyes filled with tears. "Get me out of this dress, will you, Desiree?"

I couldn't understand why Charlene took it all so seriously, why she would spend a thousand dollars for a dress just to have her picture out front. "Why does everyone want to be the star?" I asked Desiree.

"This is show business!" she exclaimed. "The Nudie-Tease isn't like the other clubs, where they're doing funny games under the table. Since Preston bought the place out, he's brought razzle-dazzle back into the Combat Zone, a real old-fashioned respect for good-looking girls."

"Preston's good to me," Charlene interjected.

"And you're good to his friends," Desiree mumbled. To me, she went on, "Preston treats all his girls fair. If you're a star, you just get it a little bit better. You get to do most of your shows on the front stage, and the DJ introduces you with some fanfare. They'll dim the lights for your slow numbers and let you control the volume of your music. You don't have to sit with the customers unless you want to. They'll put your picture in the paper and your name out front. And once you're valuable to the club, you get a little say-so about what goes on. You can have a girl fired if you don't like her. The main thing, though, is that you double your salary."

"How much do stars earn?" I asked. Preston had started me at fifty dollars a shift.

Desiree admonished me, "You don't discuss your pay with other girls. If Charlene finds out you're earning more than her, she's going to be jealous."

"I'd ask for a raise," Charlene giggled drunkenly.

"You don't talk about it," said Desiree.

As Desiree talked, I began to picture myself as the star. I imagined walking to work and seeing my name up in lights: Lolita. The men of Boston would become like Humbert Humbert, hungry for a view of my young body. The dancers would envy me. My dazzling costumes would make the men gasp. I'd receive a standing ovation after each act, and men would gather around the dressing room, hoping I'd join them for a drink.

"What do you have to do to become a star?" I asked.

" 'Many are called but few are chosen,' " Desiree said. "Of course, you need the body for it, but you've got that. Watch the girls who've made it. See how they wear their makeup, how they put their shows together. What you need is initiative. If you get good enough, Preston'll notice you."

I wanted to be a star. My palms were sweating, and I'd become acutely aware of my curly hair. Would it be considered pretty or ugly? I could wear a wig, a straight blond one, or I could straighten my hair, as I did as a child.

Desiree was still talking. "A good wardrobe is the best investment you can make in this business. That'll do more for you than anything else. I've seen mediocre-looking girls get top billing because they came to me for their costumes." She opened her suitcase to show me some samples. Checking the schedule on the wall, she said, "I tell you what. You're on in fifteen minutes. I'll let you wear one of these, to see how it feels."

Trembling with excitement, I prepared to go on stage. Having already auditioned, I knew what to expect. Still, as I'd seen at the Twilight Lounge, each show brought on a wave of stage fright, coupled with a kind of exhilaration. Although I had not yet performed to the peak of my ability, I knew I could. I felt that stripping, by allowing me twenty minutes alone on stage, gave me a chance to convince men of my beauty.

I did feel glamorous as I walked down the runway wearing Desiree's costume. Not that I accepted my own body any more than I ever had. Rather, I felt that I'd become someone else: my ideal. High up on a stage, clothed in extravagant satin and sequins, I could be tall and long-legged, the scar on my knee could disappear, my face could be smooth and ethnically unidentifiable. I measured my success in the expressions on the men's faces. They smiled. They watched me. They believed in me as the all-American girl. The skin under my sequins must be softer than the skin on their wives. One whiff of my perfume would make them as virile as when they were twenty. I controlled my own nakedness, something they desired to see, and they loved me for it. The longer I withheld it, the longer I'd keep their attention. I began to understand the rhythm of the striptease: the building of tension with the promise to remove one more piece of clothing, the small release with each removal, and the quick reharnessing of expectancy into a new tension, a new promise.

I moved with ease, almost automatically. As a teenager, I had practiced this act many times. If I were Marilyn Monroe, I had dreamed, I'd know what to do. I'd walk with my back swayed, my breasts uplifted. I'd toss my blond hair over my shoulder. The faintest of smiles would be my reward to the many men who worshiped me. I'd say no to man after man each Saturday night, knowing I could choose the best of many offers.

Marilyn Monroe existed inside me. Under the right light, she'd appear. And the rosy stage lights in the Nudie-Tease that day, dulled by cigarette smoke, refracted and bent as they reflected in the mirrors, seemed perfect. I watched myself in the mirrors that lined the walls. Each time I saw my reflection, I took another step toward conversion to the belief that I was beautiful. In the streaming light, my hair looked like a blond halo. My skin gleamed, smooth and shiny with the sweat of exertion. My legs, elongated by the mirrors' warp, looked endless and sleek.

By the end of my set, I was breathless. Small streams of sweat trickled down my sides. I carried the applause backstage with me and looked at my body. As skinny and small and curly-haired as ever, I'd just felt like a goddess. Those men were clapping for me, not for Marilyn Monroe. Or did I become someone else on stage?

A customer asked me to join him for a drink. I dressed and powdered, and then went hesitantly to his table, expecting to have to contend with his advances and propositions. But before I could ask for one drink, he ordered a bottle of champagne. He gave the waitress a large tip and asked her to leave us alone for a while.

"I can't stand them buzzing around like flies for my money," he said. "They have the erroneous impression that I'm loaded."

He did look wealthy, or at least well dressed, in tailored suit and tie. A tall man, he stooped in his chair. As I looked more closely at him, I noticed that although his face was expressive and his features mobile, his hair remained remarkably still, as if attached to something other than his scalp. Indeed, I realized, he wore a short-cropped black toupee. The young hairstyle framed a much older face. His cheeks looked hollow, his eyes held little pools of mucus and water, and his teeth had the straight yellow uniformity of dentures. Every few minutes, he coughed up a huge glob of phlegm, which he spit into a silk handkerchief. He had the hands of an old man: shaky, gnarled, and spotted with brown. Only his voice sounded young.

He handed me one of his cards. It read, "Anthony Rizzo. Attorney at Law."

"Call me Shakespeare," he said. "They all do here."

"Why's that?"

Cupping my chin in his hand, he recited:

> Shall I compare thee to a summer's day?
> Thou art more lovely and more temperate:
> Rough winds do shake the darling buds of May,
> And summer's lease hath all too short a date:
> Sometime too hot the eye of heaven shines,
> And often is his gold complexion dimm'd;
> And every fair from fair sometime declines,
> By chance or nature's changing course untrimm'd;
> But thy eternal summer shall not fade
> Nor lose possession of that fair thou ow'st;
> Nor shall Death brag thou wand'rest in his shade,
> When in eternal lines to time thou grow'st:
> So long as men can breathe or eyes can see,
> So long lives this and this gives life to thee.

"That was beautiful," I said.

"Did you not expect to find high culture in this depraved zone?"

"That's true."

"Little Lolita," he began in a fatherly tone. "I picked you out as a college girl right away. You came trotting onto stage like you were late for a lecture." He demonstrated with his fingers on the table. Assuming a falsetto, he said, "Oh! I forgot my books. Oh, professor, will you forgive me if I show you my titties?" He resumed in his normal voice, "I know. I used to teach college."

"What did you teach?"

"It doesn't matter." He lit his pipe. "I remember when *Lolita* first came out. My daughters wouldn't come near me for weeks." His laugh turned into a gurgle; he had that much liquid in his chest and throat. "Have you read the book?"

"Of course."

"I like smart girls," he mused. "Most of them talk too much, though."

"Then you'll like me. All my life I've heard, Why are you so quiet? I'm shy."

"Is that right?" He patted my hand. Imitating Humphrey Bogart, he said, "Stick with me, sweetheart. I'll give you a real education."

We spent the afternoon together. He bought me three bottles of champagne; I poured most of it into a bucket. Even so, I became slightly tipsy. I forgot that I was at work in a strip joint, earning a "tough living." In Shakespeare's presence, I felt like a celebrated show girl, a cultured courtesan worthy of the praise and poetry of a refined gentleman. Perhaps, I thought, the very vulgarity of the strip joint, where the stylized games of social intercourse never led to real involvement, made it possible for us to talk freely. Because I knew I'd never have to get any closer to Shakespeare's toupee and dentures, I let myself see him as tall, dark-haired, and poetic. Here, in a strip joint, I'd met a man who found me both beautiful and intelligent. I'd been seen. I knew I wouldn't want to bring him into my everyday life, but I believed that this rehearsal, in a place that stood somewhere between my real life and my fantasies, would strengthen me.

Shakespeare collected his hat, coat, and cane to leave. "Be here next week, same time," he said. "You're my girl, even if you are short." Then he slipped some cash into my hand.

Trying to make sense of his last comment, I waited until he left to open my hand. Then, in my palm, I found one hundred dollars. For what? I'd spent the afternoon being complimented, serenaded, and entertained. There had been no struggle to defend my purity, no push to sell drinks. Working at the Nudie-Tease seemed easy.

"You just met one of the top lawyers for the local underworld," the waitress informed me. "He'll be back next week. Once he finds a girl he likes, he stays with her. Don't push him. Let him call the shots, and he'll do good by you."

The differences between the clubs I'd worked at I attributed to the owners, or rather, to the men who posed up front as owners (I'd heard rumors of a whole bevy of unnamed men who collected profits but preferred to remain unseen). At the Twilight Lounge, Harry Chester's personality dominated. Preston Cara's character flavored the Nudie-Tease.

In the months after I met him, I realized that Preston brought a keen intelligence to his dealings in the Combat Zone. He had earned a graduate degree from one of the nation's most prestigious universities, and then, it appeared, decided to chuck it all and become a strip-joint operator. He had developed a well-rationalized analysis of the strip joint and his role in it. He believed that he offered women a chance to better themselves. A shrewd and rational dancer, he claimed, would turn the adulation of the male clientele into a manipulative sort of power. She would meet a plumber to fix her pipes, a store owner to give her a discount on clothing. In a society where "the doors are rapidly closing," a young woman could save enough money to put herself through school, learn a trade, or start a business. She might meet a sugar daddy, a man who would lift her out of her social class. She might have to sleep with him, but isn't that the way the world works? Preston offered the Nudie-Tease to girls who might otherwise live impoverished, destitute lives on the streets. For women who felt unattractive, a few months of attention from men at the Nudie-Tease could lead to self-confidence and self-respect. They'd gain access to a large pool of men, and thus sharpen their conversational skills and wit. They'd experience an economic freedom they might never see otherwise. And society would benefit at the same time. "The Nudie-Tease," Preston told me, "serves as an outlet for people whose sexuality is

60

repressed in one way or another." By providing that outlet, he thought he helped to prevent antisocial behavior, such as rape and other crimes of violence. Because of the strip joint's intrinsic social value, and because it represented a rich business opportunity for a daring few, its reputation ought to be raised to the level of other legal businesses, other places where people went to appreciate the female form, such as museums and art schools. And so Preston campaigned for legitimacy, inside and outside the club. Inside the club, he insisted that the dancers must behave like "ladies." They must be well groomed and not visibly drunk. They must appear, at least, to enjoy their jobs. Outside the club, he advertised the "All-Nude College Girl Revue" and encouraged his employees to speak out in the newspapers and on television about the essentially wholesome nature of their work.

Preston did not run a haphazard business. He scrutinized every physical and social detail of the Nudie-Tease. He wanted the bars set up just so, with the cash registers spaced ten feet apart, to ensure the bartenders' honesty and efficiency. He hired bartenders who had recently graduated from college, dark-haired young men with trimmed mustaches and muscles enough to calm a riot but not to incite one. He insisted that the music play continuously throughout the day; even a two-minute pause could send a valued customer away in a fit of impatience. Preston wanted a "clean" club. He wanted to recapture the flavor of the old Howard, where a guy and his girl could go for a spicy date in 1962. He picked his dancers carefully, to maintain a favorable mixture of body types, personalities, class and educational backgrounds. Lest they get lazy, he provided dancers with incentives to work harder: carefully meted out raises in pay and status.

His strategies worked. Undoubtedly, the Nudie-Tease compared favorably to the Twilight Lounge; I felt safe there. Still, I never liked or trusted Preston. He used his large vocabulary to intimidate uneducated women. Terribly moody, he lashed out at his employees with venom, and then expected to be forgiven without apology minutes later. He never explained his edicts; he merely issued them. He'd compliment my hairstyle one day, insult it the next, when I had done nothing to alter it in the interim. Instinctively, I knew not to confide in him, even though I felt special when he'd call me over to the managers' table to ask me how I liked work so far, to tell me that I was an attractive girl and that I should spend more time perfecting my appearance. I'd look into his clear-skinned, small-featured face, hear his well-modulated voice pronounce articulate sentences, and begin to feel mesmerized. I'd want to thank him for offering me a job in his wonderful club, where I could earn the money and attention I wanted. But then I'd stop and think that despite his words and his polished style, Preston also gave power to men like Victor, and that said something about Preston's own values.

Preston often ruled in absentia; he'd hired Victor to manage the club. Vic came from South Boston, a working-class Irish Catholic section of the city. For years, gangs of South Boston teenagers had terrorized black students bused into the area to attend the public schools; they had defined and patrolled the borders of their turf. While people from South Boston were not uniquely culpable for the charged atmosphere of racial tension in Boston, they carried a portion of the blame. Victor, however, was uniquely responsible for the level of racial tension in the Nudie-Tease. He brought to work his concept of turf, and no one dared to challenge his supremacy in the club.

Shorter than most men, Victor built up his strength by boxing. First in the military, later in prison, he gained the physical ability and the cunning to defeat two, three, even four men larger than himself in a fight. And he fought often. If a dancer complained that a customer grabbed her breast, Victor would lift that man by his collar, bang his head against the wall, and toss him out into the street. If a group of men brought too much drunk enthusiasm from a baseball game to the

Nudie-Tease, Victor would quiet them with a few deft blows.

But Victor didn't only fight the men who posed a real threat to the dancers or patrons of the club. He also attacked men who were helpless in some way: old, drunk, crippled. I once saw him punch a mentally retarded man so hard that the man reeled; drunk and somewhat unruly, the man had been yelling obscenities at the dancers.

Even more virulently, Victor sought out black men as his opponents. He apparently regretted that blacks could come into the Zone at all, and he sabotaged their freedom of movement.

Several months after I came to work at the Nudie-Tease, I saw a young black man named Leon sitting at the bar. I knew him from the university. We were both surprised, and slightly embarrassed, to see each other in this setting. After we talked for a few minutes, he got up to leave. Apparently not ready to go until he saw one more woman get naked, he stood with his empty beer in his hand, next to the managers' table. Victor looked up at him several times. When I saw Victor stand up and check his fly, as he always did before a fight, I sensed danger.

I considered warning Leon that Victor was dangerous, but something stopped me. I feared Victor myself, although I'd never seen him hit a woman. I didn't want to lose my job. On some level, I didn't believe that the violence about to occur would be real. It happened around me all the time, and if I chose not to look at it, it didn't touch me. I didn't have a husband coming home with a fractured skull because he'd gotten into trouble in the Combat Zone.

Leon may have said something to trigger Victor's rage. He probably didn't. Within a minute, Victor had him down on the floor, and was grinding his boot into Leon's face. Each time Leon tried to sit up, Victor kicked him down again. Bleeding and shrieking in terror, Leon tried to cover his face with his hands.

When Leon's face was good and bloody, Victor stopped. Leon stood up, disoriented, and looked around. The dancers and bar help all watched him, none of us offering to help. "You can't do this to me," he said.

"What you say, boy?" Victor began to slap and push him.

At that point, I yelled, "Victor, he's my friend. Leave him alone!"

Victor ignored me. Catching hold of Leon, who had been edging toward the door, preparing to run, Victor grabbed a chair and brought it down repeatedly over Leon's head. "You want to die here, nigger?" he shouted. With the chair overhead, he chased Leon out of the bar.

Everyone in the club returned to work. The customers continued to drink their beers, looking relieved that the unpleasant distraction had ended. The dancer on stage had never stopped dancing. A real professional, Rebel had continued her long-legged strut from one end of the runway to the other, and her smile had not faltered.

Rebel's mother, Virginia, stood behind the bar. Up from Georgia a month earlier, she'd needed work, and Rebel had used her relatively high status at the club to get her mother a job as a bartender. "You sure do feel protected in here," Virginia said loudly, as if to convince herself. "That's my little girl up on stage, and I don't have to worry a lick about her."

Another dancer agreed, "Victor's just protecting us."

I tried to justify the violence to myself. When a man entered the Combat Zone, I reasoned, he gave up his rights as a citizen. Here, another kind of "justice" took over, and any customer willingly took that risk. He entered a war zone, where the sight of blood drew no pity or shock from bystanders, only a kind of contempt for bad luck or weakness. Somehow, I couldn't shake the feeling that I'd seen something terribly wrong. Growing up in the South, I'd heard of many incidents, some not that far in the past, in which black men were accused of raping, attacking, or "recklessly eyeballing" white women. When a black man ended up dead in a river, or hanging from a tree, people said the murderers had defended the purity of white women. I didn't feel protected in the South, and I still didn't, in the Nudie-Tease. What kind of white woman warranted Victor's protection? What did I owe him in return?

I went backstage to the DJ booth to think about what had happened. Vita Price, the DJ, sat there spinning records. She looked engrossed in her work. I wondered why Preston had hired her, a very light-skinned black woman. Or maybe she wasn't black; she could have been Spanish.

"Did you see that?" I asked.

"See what?" She seemed uninterested.

"Victor just beat the shit out of a young black guy, for no reason."

"Yeah, I saw it. So what? Happens all the time."

"Don't you get mad?"

Vita turned around and stared at me for a minute. She said, "Don't bring your liberal bullshit to me. You think I need to hear, 'Oh, ain't it so hard to be black,' from you? I'm here for one reason and one reason only: to feed my son. You see my hair? Isn't it straight? You see my eyes? With the help of a little makeup, don't they slant up like any Chinese girl's? As far as the management here is concerned, I'm Oriental, and I want to keep it that way, you understand?"

"Isn't it hard to keep up the disguise?"

"Is your real name Lolita? I don't know one woman in here showing her real face. And you got good reason not to, because if you're so sensitive you're going to die every time you see Victor beating up on somebody."

"I know what you mean. Part of me didn't even flinch when I saw him kicking that guy. Lolita accepts it. She's got a whole different set of values from me."

"That's right," Vita said. "I could get very angry at the way they treat black women in here, but it doesn't pay. Every black dancer in here is a token, here today, gone tomorrow. She can't be too dark, and her hair can't be too nappy. The one black feature performer here was passing for Spanish. And Victor, he's just the muscle behind it. The worst racism comes from the top down, from Preston; anything black makes him highly upset. Black costumes turn him off."

Vita was older than most of the women at the Nudie-Tease, nearing thirty, and she looked too thin to be healthy. As soon as she finished one cigarette, she lit up another. Her cough shook her whole body.

"One thing's for sure," she continued. "I will not be defeated. And I won't be changed by working here, either. The other day, I just happened to be wearing a Nudie-Tease T-shirt, and I ran into a religious-minded gentleman I know. He goes, 'Nudie-Tease Nightclub. You work there?' 'Yes,' I say, 'I'm the DJ there.' He starts getting excited, 'A woman like you? A churchgoing woman! That's WRONG!' I say, 'Excuse me, are you paying to keep me and my son going?' That shut him up. Anybody who bothers to look can see I'm not doing anything wrong. I've got a BA in radio broadcasting, and I couldn't find a job. When I was pregnant, I worked as a chambermaid, a blueprint technician, a clerk in a department store. Each place fired me as soon as they found out I was pregnant. All I wanted to do was find an apartment, furnish it, and provide a home for my child."

"Where was the father?"

"He was no kind of help. Our first child died. I was on the verge of death myself when our son was born. Then my apartment was broken into, I was raped, all these things. All my son's father could say was, 'Why don't you go home?' "

"Does he help you out now?" I asked.

"Oh, sure, he comes by when he wants to, not when I need him. That's why I'm very hard on men today. Men have told me I am the pimp. I pimp men. If they've got some money, I'll talk to them, and that doesn't mean I'll give anything in return. Men say I'm hard and they say I'm cold. I have my own

66

little world that involves just my son and me. I've seen too many women fall in love with these ding-a-lings. Their children are hungry, they're hungry, and the man won't go out there and get any food. Well, I work. I pay the rent. I'm living my own life, darling, and no man's going to defeat me." She paused to put on a record. "You understand now why I didn't see any fight out there before? You're Lolita, I'm Oriental, and everything's cool, all right? There's a position opening up for head DJ, and I intend to get it."

FOUR

VENUS DE MILO
NEVER HAD IT SO GOOD

Like a talented revivalist preacher, Rebel could work her audience into a frenzy. Her steps became her words, and men believed what she said. She preached strength, and her legs were pure muscle. Have faith in symmetry and softness, her breasts seemed to say. Her crooked but steady smile promised, Through suffering you'll find redemption. She began her sermon by strutting to the far end of the runway. The congregation began to sway. "She's so fine." Back down at the fat end of the T-shaped runway, she leaned with her arms outstretched against the black backdrop. "Do it, baby." She tossed her dark hair back, a move that drew a plaintive moan from the audience. And then she made her first offering: breasts. "Oh God!" They stood out white against her body, still browned from the summer sun. "Yes!" She whirled in fast circles until dizzy. "Take me with you!" In a tense and solemn moment, she removed her G-string. Not a sound could be heard as the men stared at the tiny mound of hair, shaved into a heart shape, between her legs. The spirit touched one man, who shook and jerked his arm up and down a few last strokes, until a relief, release, an outpouring of devotion came in white spurts, and he was ousted just at the climactic moment by Victor, who punished those who had so little faith that they could not wait until they were alone to declare their undying love for the body so naked and close and untouchable in front of them. "I didn't know what I was doing," the man cried out. Rebel looked away, as if to say, The strong in faith accept their fate.

I sat with Rebel's mother, Virginia, watching the performance. "She's perfect," Virginia sighed. "Venus de Milo never had it so good."

"You don't mind all these guys looking at her?" I asked.

Virginia shook her head. "I've got confidence in my girl. I've seen her handle guys. She'll just jump up and cuss them out in full living color. She's been known to pour beer over them, their beer and her drink that they paid seven dollars for, right in their face, for saying something vulgar."

It was true. Rebel had a reputation in the club for putting up with little flak from the customers. She often used her status as a rising star to insist that men who troubled her be thrown out of the bar. A southerner, she had strong beliefs about how a lady should be treated. She also had very definite convictions about how a lady should act. Forever scolding other dancers about sitting with their legs apart, or not wearing enough perfume to cover the inherently offensive odors of their bodies, she was determined to ameliorate the image of the stripper. She wanted the dancers of the Nudie-Tease to be known worldwide as clean and wholesome. We were not whores, but performers. She believed, without any apparent doubt, in the premise of the strip joint. It would bring her fame. It would bring her adoration. She wanted to be the star performer, and she was willing to crush anyone who threatened her success. At present, she was vying for top billing against several other dancers, Charlene among them.

"Rebel is a prude," Virginia said after some thought. "She always has been. Of all my four girls, she was the one who didn't like arguing, didn't like anybody wearing her clothes. She was everything a mother could want in a little girl. She loved the color pink; everything had to be pink. She looked like a little cloud of powder coming out of the bathroom."

"And she ended up as a stripper," I said.

Virginia got defensive. "Rebel has always been a morally straight girl. I thought she'd be a nun. Her home life had nothing to do with stripping."

"I didn't mean anything by that," I apologized. "I guess I'm a little jealous of your relationship with each other."

Virginia warmed up to me. "Nobody can understand it. Sometimes, out of the dark in here, I'll hear this voice, 'Ma, come here.' All the heads turn. Mother! What's a mother doing in the Combat Zone? All these guys ask me out, and Rebel will come over and say, 'That's my mama. You better leave her alone.'"

"Rebel's protective of you?"

"That's right. She likes having me here. At first, she was embarrassed to have me see her, until I made one statement. I said, 'Who do you think used to clean that thing? I know everything you got.' I know her whole story, and I know her doing this is just a matter of survival instinct."

"I wish my mother could see it that way."

"Now, I didn't exactly pick it out as her vocation when she was little. I wanted each of my girls to follow their own talents. But they didn't really get a chance. I didn't have a chance myself to get them off on a good footing. I've been divorced since Rebel was six years old, and their father, he was a drunk who never even paid child support. I had to make a go of it myself."

"That must be where Rebel learned to go after what she wants," I said, watching Rebel's determined strut across the stage.

"I can't blame her. I've worked in sewing factories and gotten lint in my eyes and in my chest, and even coughed blood. There she was. She left home at sixteen, because I couldn't get her the things she wanted. She followed this girl up to Boston. Rebel didn't even have a high school education; there wasn't too much she could do. She has a terrific figure. It's easy money. I don't blame her one bit."

"Did you know what she was doing, back then?" I thought of my own situation at sixteen, my conflicting desires to tell and keep from my parents what I was doing.

"You got to understand one thing about Rebel: she can take care of herself. I knew that. When she was only thirteen, she begged me to let her go out and find a job. I said, 'No, Rebel, no one will hire you. There's child labor laws.' Well, she went out and got her a job managing a restaurant. She said she was sixteen. They knew she wasn't, and that's why they paid her below minimum wage. Her feet were a mass of red blisters, and she kept on going to school and maintaining a B-plus average all throughout that time. So I knew that Rebel could take care of herself, and I didn't have to ask what she was doing. When she told me, I understood. She's done the best she could from the background she came from."

Rebel waved to us from the stage. "Hey, Mama." Startled, a few men looked from mother to daughter.

"That's my baby," Virginia said proudly. "Seeing as how she borrowed my plane fare back to Georgia, I think she wants her mama here to help straighten her up. Rebel's a good girl, but somehow she got herself mixed up with the wrong kind of guy. He's using her to buy cocaine for him. Even though Rebel would never do any herself, she's got him hanging on her like a leech. He flat told me when I got here that I'm messing with his livelihood. I told him he's messing with my daughter, and he better watch out, because deep down in her heart she's a mama's girl. I'm going to get her away from him. It says in the Bible the homing instinct is the strongest part of a woman's life, and men stray like tomcats. As soon as Skippy strays away, I'm going to snatch my little girl back."

On stage, Rebel began her floor show. The audience fell silent as she got down on the floor and lifted her legs. Just before she spread her legs, she covered herself with her hand. One man moaned, "Come on, move the hand." That she would not do. She'd show everything else, but she chose to keep private this one part of her anatomy.

"She does it with a lot of class," Virginia mused. "She's butt naked, rolling around like a tumblebuck, and it doesn't even seem nasty. See that, her hand is strategically placed. She's a real lady."

People forever discussed the floor show at the Nudie-Tease. The customers cherished it. The bosses encouraged it. The dancers struggled with the idea of it; we debated whether it was sensuous or obscene. We concurred that the female body, graceful and lovely, ought to be admired. Some dancers felt that the floor show afforded the possibility for healthy admiration. With romanticized imagery, they described the dance as a kind of ballet performed by innocent fawns. They marveled at the movement of sculptured limbs. They described the gestures of extension and withdrawal as a picturesque rendition of the sexual act itself. The floor show paid homage to the vagina, the clitoris, the crux of female sensuality.

Other dancers argued that the floor show, in its very admiration of the female body, separated out one section of the body in a rather artificial way. Why should our crotches be loved any more than our armpits? They wanted the dance to flow more evenly from one stage of undress to another, with no special emphasis on the last few moments of nudity.

Still other dancers saw in the floor show's conceptual severing of the genitals from the rest of the body a theme of domination and submission. To them the scenario of the strip-tease looked like this: the woman offers her body for the viewing pleasure of the man. He watches, with full knowledge of what will happen. No matter what, the woman on stage will undress for him within a few minutes. She may be the most beautiful woman, a woman who would not look twice at him in the real world, and she will still take off her clothes for him. She may tease and taunt and parade around as if she is unattainable, but the fact is that she is going to take her clothes off. She can be proud and defiant, but the bitch is going to take her clothes off. Finally, she gets down on the floor and submits to what she's been asking for all along: visual rape. In this conventional view of rape, the red-blooded male acts on his uncontrollable lust, and punishes the slut by giving her exactly what she deserves.

My friend Patrice often spoke of the floor show as a kind of invasion. "It's like there's this big Picasso and all they see is his signature," she said. "It puzzles me when they look up into my crotch like that. Is it like a chimney and if they look far enough they'll see daylight at the top? What are they looking for? Even during sex they don't see it. I've yet to see anyone fuck with their eyeballs. I don't want their eyes inside me like that."

No matter how we conceived of it, we all justified, rationalized, or rejected the floor show on some grounds. The one part of our job that absolutely distinguished us from other performers, the floor show brought us dangerously close to being like prostitutes. In it, we acknowledged that our most valued commodities were our genitals. To see them, men left their homes, risked their marriages, and frequented low-life establishments. Most of us did not like to think in these terms. We liked to think of ourselves as show girls, professional dancers, social workers performing a needed service. We wanted to see ourselves as "good girls." Admittedly, we worked at a job the larger society labeled as bad. Still, we had control over one part of our act if no other: the floor show. Thus we invested it with symbolic meaning. Each of us developed a private morality about it. We imposed limitations on ourselves, the transgression of which would make us plummet into "bad girl" status. Some women would not do a floor show at all. Others would lie on the floor but not lift their legs. Others, like Rebel, would spread their legs but cover themselves with their hands. Still others would show everything but refuse to move their hips. And even those dancers who seemed to love the rug with sexual abandon justified their lewdness: they felt no passion, did not get turned on, only acted the part. If the society saw us as loose women, we knew that our standards were as rigid, if outwardly different, as any nun's.

I got up to dance after Rebel's set ended. I felt like a non sequitur; our two acts could not have been more dissimilar. She played a rambunctious but proper lady. I played a little girl. Like all of the dancers, we played roles we'd learned in the outside world. The Nudie-Tease had a plethora of good girls and bad girls, ice queens, seductresses, and so on. We'd practiced these roles since childhood. When we stood on stage at the Nudie-Tease, with the mandate to act sexy, we portrayed sexiness in the only ways we knew how. We exaggerated and isolated the elements of sexiness we'd always known to make sure that they came across clearly.

Some dancers approached this process more deliberately than others. Patrice, who was an actress, always said that she welcomed the chance to "try on a character." She grew up a middle-class kid in a row house in Delaware; now she could come into work and be an extraterrestrial, the Queen of England, a Latin American revolutionary. "Men don't come to see me, anyway," she said. "They come to be handed a fantasy, a plastic-wrapped shrink, whore, wife, mother, baby-sitter, mistress, consultant." With remarkable precision, Patrice could imitate the speech and mannerisms of any character she chose. Committed to the accuracy of her presentation, she would apply and reapply her makeup throughout the day, until finally she had sweated part of it off, smeared more of it, and looked like she wore a garish Greek tragic mask, a caricature of her real face. Each day, she'd critique her own performance. "Cleopatra didn't gel, not completely. I'll try Helen of Troy tomorrow." The next day, she'd wear white robes, a tiara made from tinfoil, and speak about the fleet of ships on its way. Although each character she created seemed utterly convincing, she insisted that she could not stop her search until she found the one role that suited her.

Not every dancer had the talent or desire to create a separate character as convincing as Patrice's, but almost every dancer assumed a false name. These names gave us some degree of anonymity. Some dancers chose names that suggested characters who were like a natural extension of their real selves. Others picked the names of their idols, women who seemed so different from them that only a magical leap, like a change in identity, could bridge the gap. There were the little girl names, such as Babydoll, or my Lolita. Other women named themselves after delectable, sweet morsels of food: Sugar, Honey, Cookie, Brandy, Cinnamon, Tangerine, Ginger. Some of the names professed a more rebellious spirit: Rebel, Scarlett, Stormy Night. Foreign names, especially French names, appeared frequently, and implied that the dancer was really "exotic": Chantal, Nicole, Inge, Monique, Angelique. Still other names brought to mind exotic scents: Jasmine, Violet, Lavender. Gentle animals could be namesakes: Fawn, Swan, Kitty. Movie stars and fairy-tale women figured large on the roster: Farrah, Lana, Cinderella, Princess.

I played Lolita, and for a reason. I could circumvent my shyness by attributing it to this other personality, this borrowed character. My Lolita was an all-American girl who had no concept of her sexiness, who must have been led blindly to the stage, because she didn't seem to realize the implications of what she was doing. Too naïve to be manipulative, she presented no threat to men; they could feel wise, knowing, and a little naughty when they watched her. She, as a child, did not need to feel too responsible for her actions.

I began my set seconds after Rebel ended her floor show. The men still looked hopeful. Would Rebel break the rule of the twenty-minute set and perform an encore in which she compassionately moved her "strategically placed" hand? Initially, I felt a vague wave of disgust for these men. They seemed more rabid than appreciative. Yet, by the time I reached the end of the runway, I had suspended my ability to judge them. The anger I often felt offstage when I thought about the inequities of this situation in which men watched while women supplicated disappeared into the force of my desire to be admired. Whatever the cost, I wanted these men to like me. It didn't matter who they were. I preferred not to see them, in fact, because I realized that they could not possess the great qualifications for judgment with which I endowed them. Instead of looking at their faces, I looked at the walls, into the mirrors, over their heads. I tried to harness my disparate thoughts into one compelling, pleasant strand of memory:

I thought about Lamont, the man I had met in school several weeks earlier. We had noticed each other, first in the cafeteria, then in the library, and I had begun to fantasize about him. I'd pictured him in an old New England three-decker house, baking bread and writing poetry. He'd be eminently available and instantly infatuated with me. Not wanting to seem too aggressive, I'd plotted ways to meet him. I could follow him into class registration and then sign up for whatever classes he chose. I could spend the afternoon at the school bus depot; when he showed up, I could quietly slip into the seat next to him. But he was probably married; he looked to be in his early thirties. If not, he probably wouldn't want to go out with a stripper. I associated him with the small leftist contingent on campus. He wore the obligatory beard and Indian print shirts of that group; he ate in the health food restaurant on campus. I, too, was a fringe member of that group, although I was hesitant to become too involved; I anticipated rejection if I told people what I did for a living.

I'd seen Lamont at the rally to support the teachers' union, then at the demonstration to keep the ROTC off campus. I'd even managed to sit next to him when a group of concerned students met to discuss the administration's racist admission and hiring practices. Lamont, himself black, hadn't noticed me at all during that meeting. During those two hours, he'd spoken forcefully. The anger and eloquence in his voice had commanded attention. He'd spoken of "the struggle" and "the movement" in a way I hadn't heard since my childhood, among my parents and their friends in the civil rights movement. After the meeting, I'd heard someone say that he had been a conscientious objector during the Vietnam War. My fantasy had grown larger. Here was a man with my own beliefs, who spoke with intelligence and passion, and whom I had never seen with a woman.

One day, he introduced himself to me. "I've seen you around," he said. "My name is Lamont." He came from Los Angeles, where he'd grown up with adopted parents. Now they had died, and he had no family, other than a born-again Christian sister who hadn't really trusted him ever since he'd refused to serve God and his country in the war. He spoke quietly, but with the same force as he spoke in public. In the course of an hour, he told me of numerous situations in which he had been helpless or misunderstood. He survived each time by resisting, nonviolently. He presented each case with such a sense of indignation to have been in the right and been wronged that I wanted to stand up and defend him, in whatever cause. I wanted to grab the whip his father had used to beat him when he was twelve, to rip the badges off the racist cops who put him in jail for the possession of a small quantity of marijuana, to scream some sense into the Jewish parents of his ex-wife who continually pressured him to convert and get circumcised. Susceptible to the case of any underdog, I felt for him even more intensely because he was gentle, and because I'd never seen a man so beautiful. He was very dark-skinned and wore a bright knit cap, woven with the colors of the Ethiopian flag: red, green, and gold. He looked thin and muscular. I shivered when I imagined his long, slender fingers touching me.

Trusting him because he had been frank, and testing him to see if he would still like me if he knew, I said, "I work as a stripper."

Every other man I'd told that to had either asked to come see me perform, insinuated that I must be sexually insatiable, or somehow condemned me as immoral. Lamont asked simply, "What's it like?"

I felt that he acknowledged my daring and my differentness, and that he also understood my need to put myself in the most hostile environment and wage a struggle for survival there. I became like his comrade in struggle, an underdog myself. Talking to him, I got a picture of the strip joint as a place where many forces sought to destroy me, and where I, defiant and strong of purpose, resisted. Exactly what my purpose there was, I didn't know. Even if it was as mundane as to earn good money in tight times, it felt like a cause and he seemed to support it.

Back at the Nudie-Tease, my first song ended. The men clapped politely as I stepped behind the curtain. I had danced for them for nearly five minutes and had barely seen them. I knew that the bar was less than half full. I'd spotted Bert, a customer of mine, sitting behind the second register. The rest of the men seemed like a typical afternoon crowd: a few bald heads, a few suits and ties, a few blue collars. Although I'd hardly seen them, I wanted to please them. As usual, I played a game with myself on stage. If I could be sure that I had the men's full attention at the beginning of each song, then I would allow myself the luxury of getting lost in my memory. If I did not perform with zeal, if their indifferent expressions did not turn into smiles, or at least vague expressions of interest, then I would have to extend my effort throughout the whole song.

I'd always start my set with the song "You're Sixteen." As Lolita, I skipped, ran, and jumped. Lolita never walked like a grown-up, and she surely never strutted like a stripper who knew that she was sexy. No, Lolita looked surprised all the time. Each time she bent over and lifted up her dress, she looked naughty, not purposely seductive. She grinned, she winked, she stood with her hands on her hips in mock exasperation when she tried to unsnap a recalcitrant brassiere. She giggled and pointed to her breasts, as if she, too, were seeing them for the first time, and found them an amusing addition to her prepubescent anatomy. She carried balloons and popped them, or brought her baby doll on stage with her. Every now and then she struck a sophisticated pose, and then laughed at herself, to show that it had been accidental, a foreshadowing of nascent sexuality. Her garters and fishnet stockings clashed with her pigtails and demeanor, and when she sat on a chair to remove her stockings with exaggerated formality, it became clear that she was a little girl set free in her mother's dressing room, not a French whore making a ritual of her dishabille.

This day, I skipped out from behind the curtain to the strains of my second song, "My Boy Lollipop." Stopping in front of an older man, I pointed my toes in, like a scared little schoolgirl, and pouted. Slowly, reluctantly, he smiled. Then I let my hips rotate freely, as if I had no control over them. I gasped and pretended to stop them, but they wouldn't stop. The men all laughed. As I ran to the end of the runway, I saw their eyes follow me. I could return to my thoughts.

After our first date, Lamont brought me to his house. He did have an old three-decker, but not on a tree-lined street. One of the local universities had gobbled up all the property on the block, only to tear down the houses and set up parking lots. Lamont's house remained, because in it he found a cause, and he refused to sell out. Inside, the house seemed gloomy, barely lived in. "My ex-wife took half of the furniture," he explained. She had left six months earlier, and he was just recovering. He hadn't been with a woman since then.

I had already decided that I would spend the night with him. I liked him very much, and did not want to risk never seeing him again because of some newfound prudishness that I'd gained during my year at the Nudie-Tease. He, however, did not insist on getting to know me in that way. He offered to drive me home after our herb tea. "No," I was forced to say out loud, "I want to spend the night with you."

In his room, we kissed tentatively. His lips were soft. His hair smelled faintly of coconut oil. Blinded in the darkness, I ran my fingers across his face, feeling the bony protrusion of his high cheekbones, the broad incline of his nose, the forthright jut of his chin beneath his beard. He took my hands and kissed them. I felt a coiled spring of desire release itself and surge up my spine. When he unbuttoned my shirt, his hair brushed my skin lightly. His chest was damp and smooth, almost hairless. I traced the outlines of his nipples with my fingers. My own nipples were pushing out against the restraining fabric of my bra as he moved his tongue slowly from my neck to my belly and back again. He sat on the bed, while I stood in front of him, my hands reaching into his black entwined hair. He reached back to unsnap my bra, and as it fell, he cupped my breasts in his hands and kissed them, first one, then the other. My knees became weak, and I pushed him back on the bed, my body over his.

"Take off the bra!" a man at the Nudie-Tease yelled. "Let's go." He leaned over the bar, his face expectant. I had unsnapped my bra, but had not yet shown my breasts. My second song would end in less than a minute. Now was the time. I took it off quickly, then covered my breasts with my hands. My breasts bounced beneath my hands as I walked.

"Come on," the man begged. "Let us see them."

I took my hands away for a few seconds before running backstage. The men clapped.

For my third number, I pulled out a high-backed chair and sat in it with deliberately overstated poise. I crossed and uncrossed my legs several times before starting to bare them. I chose one man in the audience to gaze at romantically as I pretended to discover for the first time the mechanics of a garter belt. With that done, I peeled back the black nylon to reveal my pale skin. The men murmured approvingly. I moved off the chair, down the runway, and back into my real scene of seduction.

Lamont's hands felt warm on my body. Every inch of skin he touched felt heated and colored with excitement. We moved naked on top of the sheets, touching skin and lips. We raised more and more passion and sounds and sighs from our caresses, until, finally, I was breathless, and still his tongue drew more pleasure from me. And then we moved together, in a rhythm we both knew, our hands clasped at the top of the bed, every part of us touching. Somehow, for the first time, I knew that I could let my mind stay with my body, that I did not need to create a gulf between the encroaching physical ecstasy and my feeling self, and I began to release myself to an intensity of passion that far surpassed sensation, and led me to cry out, "I love you!"

Again, the voices at the Nudie-Tease brought me back. "Now she'll show something," a man said. "Do you think she's a real blonde?"

A hush fell over the bar as I removed my G-string. Even the men who had watched my show with little interest now turned to see if I would do a floor show. An older man put on his glasses and stared at me with a new precision. A well-dressed man, perhaps a lawyer or accountant, extended and flicked his tongue, as if that motion would incite the spread-eagled abandon he desired from me.

Lolita always left me alone and conflicted before a floor show. On the one hand, I felt a tremendous power to attract and hold the attention of the men in the audience. At this point in my act more than any other, I became female, in an animal sense. By virtue of my gender, I could turn heads, quicken pulses, and harden penises. I no longer had to try to seduce; this was *it*, the bounty given to the men who endured all the preliminaries. I wanted to reward them, to spread my legs and show them the part of my flesh they valued more than any other.

But I also felt a certain fear. What if my coveted treasure did not please them? If the sight of my genitals left their heartbeats slow, their penises soft, I would have no other means of gaining their attention.

True, I could move in ways that would remind them of times they had made love, and maybe that, rather than my body, would stay their interest. But probably not. Floor shows at the Nudie-Tease were not meant to have the fluidity of lovemaking. Instead, they consisted of a series of still poses, designed to show glimpses of the genitals from different angles. They were not meant to be sexual, as such. The transitions from one pose to another did not follow the movements of sex, but were like the still-life poses found on the pages of girlie magazines. In the etiquette of the classy strip joint, a floor show that looked too much like actual sex was considered vulgar. A good floor show would intimate the possibility of sex by showing the sex organs. If a dancer moved too much during a floor show, a man would have to accept her version of the sexual act, because there she'd be enacting it. However, if she displayed an aesthetically pleasing series of poses, a man could take what she offered and fit it into his own fantasy. If he liked her vagina, and, less importantly, the legs, breasts, and ass around it, he could have what he came for: a fantasy. Nothing she did could alter his opinion at that point. He'd either take or reject her body for his fantasies. I had observed half of an audience leave when a new dancer, who had not yet learned the etiquette of the floor show, writhed passionately against the rug as if it were a man. That same audience had looked with rapt attention at a dancer who calmly spread her legs.

If I wanted to keep the attention of the men, I could do no more than remove my G-string and let them look at me. What I had between my legs would either please them or displease them. Their judgment was beyond my control. If I did not do a floor show, I would surely lose half my audience, but at least they would not have left because they saw me and found me wanting. To be left after showing myself seemed like the most painful judgment, yet showing myself also offered me the only chance to know whether or not I had been accepted. Each time I performed, I had to weigh the pains and rewards of each option, and choose one. I usually chose to do a floor show.

Looking from man to man to see their reactions, I began my floor routine. I stretched out on the rug, my legs together. First I raised and extended one leg, then the other. I twisted, stretched, held the pose, released it. I arched my back and pointed my toes. To the men on each side of the bar, I exposed myself. They seemed to like it. The older fellow with the glasses leaned as far forward as he could without climbing over the bar. The man with the flicking tongue continued to probe the air as if it were his mistress. I felt successful, until I saw one man gather his coat and newspaper and leave the bar. He might have had to rush off to work at the end of his lunch hour, or suddenly remembered that he left his kettle on his stove, or left for any number of reasons, but I still felt abandoned.

I tried to shift back into my memories. I could not evoke the pleasant image of Lamont again. Instead, an earlier scene appeared vividly in front of me:

I often spent the weekend at Grandma's house. I was ten years old. She had just moved from New York to join us in the South. In New York, she'd lived in a section of Brooklyn where many old Jewish men and women like herself spoke with Yiddish accents as they congregated in lawn chairs on the pavement in front of their buildings in the summer, or when they bought only the freshest loaves of rye bread from the many competing delicatessens. She never socialized very much, but she knew her neighbors, and they always managed to find out her business. "So, you have a new grandson," I remembered the bent old woman with the blue numbers on her wrist saying when Sean was born. "He has our blessings, Sonya." Then she moved south to join us. I had never felt as completely happy as when I ran down the platform at the train station to greet her. She surrounded me with her fleshy arms and we both cried. "You've grown so tall," she said. I was the shortest person in my fifth grade class, but I'd almost reached her height already.

She moved into a three-room cottage with a porch and an exposed furnace in the living room. I imagined that it was just like the house of her grandmother in Russia, the midwife who bragged of her hundreds of children. Grandma would love it there. But after a few days, as she trudged down the muddy driveway, past the big house whose property the little cottage had been built on, past the mangy horses the family at the big house rescued from slaughterhouses to sell on the black market, past the loud and poorly clothed children of that family, she began to look miserable. She looked at the slanted way the cottage sank into the ground, the chipped paint on the outside, the stained wallpaper on the inside, and she said, "This is where I'm to stay?"

"It's not so bad, Ma," my mother said. "It's a fifteen-minute walk from the shopping mall, a fifteen-minute walk from us, it's cheap, and you'll have your privacy."

"Where will I get the foods I need?" Grandma asked. "I need certain things, you know."

She adjusted quickly. Although there was no delicatessen at the mall, she still chose her bread with care, feeling each processed loaf through its plastic wrap before choosing the freshest one. Her house she scrubbed and polished until it shone. She put a linen cloth on the table, flower arrangements on the windowsills, bright pictures on the walls. She cooked potato latkes, and the house began to smell like her. I would stop by there on my way to and from school. Often, I'd stay with her for several days at a time. I welcomed the chance to escape from my house with four children competing for

84

attention, two adults yelling about politics and how to pay the bills, and weekly phone calls from my father in New York, which were always followed by a day of silent resentment from my mother. At Grandma's, the only sounds were of her in the kitchen running water and clanging pots, or the two of us talking quietly by the furnace about God, whom she said did exist, despite my parents' Marxist claims to the contrary. I had begun to realize, with terror, that my grandmother would not live forever. That thought, within an atheist framework, left me feeling desolate.

"When I'm one hundred years old," she'd reassure me, "then I'll go to heaven."

But there was something else about her. No matter how I tried to push it out of my mind, it would resurface. She lived with a tremendous amount of fear. She usually managed to control it; periodically, it grew so large that it overwhelmed her. As a young child, I'd believed everything she said. I, too, would become terrified that the neighbors were listening to her through the walls, that the immigration officials wanted to cart her away for some crime she never committed, that my step-father was plotting to hurt my mother. By the time I was ten, I had learned to separate myself from her enough to think of explanations for her fear: she had raised a child alone in a time when no decent woman was supposed to do that; she had been a Jew in a historic period when no Jew could feel safe; she had been an object of ridicule in the factory because she persisted in being an intellectual. All of my reasoning, however, could not block out the fright I felt each time she "turned."

She gave no warning. As we chatted, she broke off small pieces of cake to soften in her tea; she had only two teeth left, and she wouldn't trust a dentist to fit her with dentures. Her gums looked pink and pretty as she smiled at me and said, "Lauri, darling, finish what's left of the cake." I ate. When I looked up expecting to see her gratified, grandmotherly expression, I shrank back in horror. Her lips had curled around her

85

last rotting teeth; her face had grown red and her nostrils flared.

"That filthy dog," she said.

"Who, Grandma?"

"He thinks he can put me back here in this shack. What am I, a slave on the plantation? I come and take care of his children, and this is what he does, hides me back here with the horse manure? I told Ruthie not to marry him."

Stupidly, I tried to defend my stepfather. "They thought you'd like this house. Mommy chose it, too."

"He has her fooled." Then she realized what I had done. I had taken sides; I had betrayed her. "You rotten child," she said. "Go back to him, go on, get out of my house."

"But Grandma," I cried, "I love you. I didn't mean anything."

"After all I did for you! I gave you the best of everything, the most expensive dolls, the best chocolates. You're like the rest of them."

"No," I protested. I felt that I had only one option: to side with her. "I hate him, too."

She eyed me to see if I meant what I said. Then she came to me and squeezed my hands. "You understand, then, why I have to be careful. You are the only one who understands me, Lauri." She looked calm again. She'd won her battle. Just what it was about, I didn't know. I did know that I had entered into some kind of a pact with her so that I could bring back the grandmother I knew.

She went back to the stove. "See what I've made for you? Little cakes, ten little cakes for you, darling." She looked plump and familiar again. "We can forget that little talk. It was foolish. You've forgotten, yes?"

I could forget that particular talk, and the others like it, if I tried, but I could not forget the fear that remained with me. I wanted to believe that Grandma, the person with whom I could feel absolutely protected, would not leave me. I wanted

86

an assurance that would supersede these ugly aberrations. "You won't ever leave me, Grandma?"

"No," she said, "but when I'm one hundred years old and I should go, these are for you." She pointed to her notebooks.

In the Nudie-Tease, I also reached for an assurance that I would not be left entirely alone. One man had left already. I searched the audience for a man whose interest I could trust. The flicking tongue. To avoid my fear, I linked myself emotionally to the most vulgar man in the audience. He wouldn't leave before my set ended. I looked directly at him as I moved from one pose to another. It almost seemed as if his tongue extended ten feet to its intended destination between my legs, because I felt a kind of relief or satisfaction or safety as I looked at its continuous, unchanging rhythm. The man looked ecstatic, and I received a long applause as I left the stage, my act completed.

FIVE

STAY AWAY!

One morning a year later, Patrice sat in the dressing room with her head in her hands. "What am I doing here?" she said. "I thought I'd be a comrade in arms with the women here. There's something about being naked together, putting up with the shit together. You'd think there'd be some recognition of that, some . . ."

"Sisterhood?" I asked. Patrice had talked about this many times before.

"Community. I look at their faces, and I can see it's just as traumatic for them as it is for me, but they deny it. It's like a fucking Tupperware party in the dressing room. Who the hell cares if your costume cost twenty dollars or two hundred dollars, or if your breasts are sagging more than they did a year ago?"

The impassioned pace and timbre of her speech made me wonder if she spoke for herself, or if she delivered the words of an invented character. I couldn't always tell with Patrice. Into every role she played she injected conviction and impulsiveness. She'd gasp for breath between words, filling silences with frenzied hand movements and facial expressions. At times, her thoughts seemed to progress without logic; she'd voice any association that occurred to her. I considered her creative, if hard to know. I hadn't yet seen the core from which all her associations flowed.

"Did something happen?" I asked.

Her voice trembled. "Did you notice anything about Charlene yesterday?"

"What do you mean?"

"What I mean is, she got so drunk she couldn't walk. I lifted her up and took her home, to her place. She lives with some guy named Charlie, but he split two days ago. They had a fight; that's why she was getting more sloshed than usual. Anyway, I figured I'd better stick her in a cold shower to sober her up a little bit. I was holding her up under the water, and I noticed some tan paint running down the drain. It was peeling off her body, and as it came off, the bruises underneath it started to show."

"Charlie beat her?" I could almost believe it. Charlie hadn't lived up to any of his promises so far.

"All I know, Lauri, is that the woman had bruises all over her body, on her legs, her arms, and she covered them up."

"What did you do? Did you talk to her about it?"

"That's what I'm ashamed of. We ended up talking about who's going to be the next star, Charlene or Rebel. I stayed over there, on the couch. The whole time, I wanted to wake her up and say, Let's really talk, but I didn't know what to say."

"What would you want to say?"

She cleared her throat and began to lecture. "I'd say, Charlene, sisterhood is the only defense we have in the Zone. Welfare's trying to take away Melon's kids because she's supporting a junkie. Cookie's seventeen and she's already been dancing for two years; everyone else she knows is either a housewife or a whore, and she didn't know what else to do. You've got bruises all over your beautiful body. We're being degraded and brutalized, and we could band together to fight it."

"I don't get it, Patrice. What are you doing in the Zone if you think you're being degraded and brutalized?"

"Money. I'm getting paid back for all the unpaid work I do in the theater."

"I'm not convinced."

"Actors need to see different slices of life."

"For two years?"

"And men need to see strong women. One look at me and they know we're more than weak little creatures." She was plump and large-breasted; Rubens would have found her perfect. Her white skin contrasted with the black hair on her head and legs. Fleshy and rounded, her thighs were also thick with muscle. Now her eyes lit up, and she spoke rapidly. "Charlene has that in her, too. She's a strong woman, if you look past the fluff."

"Why are you fixated on Charlene? Why not Sugar or Jasmine or me, for God's sake?"

Patrice lifted her hands as if to punctuate her thoughts. Then she dropped them and looked away. When she spoke, her voice was hushed and tender. "The truth? I'm in love with Charlene. I love her. You know, sometimes I watch her at the bar, with some guy sneaking a feel of her breasts and slobbering in her ear. I can't even tell you what I feel. That's her skin. Her breasts. God." She began to cry. "And now these bruises. The way I could love her, she's never known it. I'd hold her until the pain went away. I'd love her softness, not hurt it. Her skin, her breasts, her little hands." Patrice clasped her arms in front of her, as if cradling a baby.

"I knew it," Rebel's voice rang out. We hadn't heard her enter the dressing room. "A pervert."

"Hold it, Rebel," I said. "How much of our conversation did you hear?"

90

"Enough." She turned to the mirror to survey her appearance.

"If you heard the whole thing, you'd know that Patrice took Charlene home to help her out. Charlene was drunk off her ass, and Patrice slept on the couch."

"Took her home!" Rebel turned to Patrice. "Did you show her a good time?"

"You're distorting it. I'm not talking about a variation on fucking." Patrice looked unhappily down at the floor.

"Watch your language," said Rebel.

Dropping the tenderness from her voice, and retrieving her usual speed and gesticulations, Patrice said, "Women helping women. It's the only way we're going to make it in this place."

"You're the one who needs help," said Rebel. "Every day you come in here pretending you're someone else. Who are you today? Joan of Arc? Tiny Tim?"

"Nobody," Patrice answered. "In the Zone, I'm nobody." She picked up her purse and left the dressing room.

Rebel and I put on our makeup in silence. A few other dancers arrived. Gathered around the mirror, they curled their eyelashes and set their hair. When her audience included five other women, Rebel began to talk. "I suppose ya'll know about Patrice and Charlene. Charlene was drunk last night, and Patrice went on home with her. Showed her a good time. That's right, girls: a lesbian."

"You think she woke Charlene up or did it to her while she was passed out?" Tulip asked.

"Any way she could get it," a dancer namer Sugar rejoined. "A dyke's like a dog in heat." They all laughed.

Rebel brandished her curling iron like a weapon. "I'll threaten any one of them that comes near me. I can't think of anything more disgusting than two girls doing it. Lord, what is this world coming to? One day they're all buddy buddy with you. They understand your problems with your boyfriend. Yes ma'am, they've been through it themselves. And the next day they're trying to suck you in. They try to get me."

"Who, Rebel?" I asked. "How do you know the difference between someone being nice to you and someone trying to get you?"

"Let's just say I know. Reputations follow you." She smiled sweetly at herself in the mirror, her girlish expression hardly matching her words. "They try to put their hands on you. Ya'll better listen up on my position on this: Stay away!"

"Who're you talking to?" Sugar asked indignantly. "There's no lesbians in this room at the moment."

Rebel glanced at me. "You never can be too sure. Being friends with one is runner-up to being one yourself."

I wanted to defend Patrice, because I thought I understood her intentions. This characterization of her as a lecherous hag preying on the heterosexual calamities of her co-workers couldn't have been less true. But my desire to protect myself was stronger.

Like every other dancer at the Nudie-Tease, I found ways to hold myself separate. I needed to do this to assure myself that the job had not overpowered me, that I, unlike the women around me, had maintained my strength. I felt no need to defend myself against accusations of lesbianism, which I felt cast no particular aspersion on my character. But I did need to declare my invulnerability to any attack. I could not be brought down to the base level of concerns at the Nudie-Tease, I had tried to say in various ways. What basis of similarity could there be between me and the other dancers?

In some ways, the defense I built at the Nudie-Tease resembled my defense in all situations. I accented my differentness. I had learned to define my identity that way as a Jewish child in the Christian South; there, because I couldn't really change the shape of my nose or the wave of my hair, I had learned to feel all right about myself by cultivating a feeling of difference. The side effect of distancing myself enough to feel different, and thus invulnerable, was that I could not feel close to people. I isolated myself and felt lonely, but still preferred that loneliness to entrusting my self-image to others.

My earliest defense at the Nudie-Tease grew out of my interest in "natural living." To offset the dirtiness of the Zone, I wanted to make myself pure in body. If I could present a clean and radiant body to the men, as a kind of offering, I thought, then perhaps I could inspire them to care for their own bodies and their wives' bodies in a healthier way. With this in mind, I became extremely discerning about what I would eat or put on my skin. I ate a vegetarian diet and restricted my intake to organically grown products with no preservatives or refined sugar. I refused to wear polyester or nylon; only cotton, silk, or wool could touch my skin. The makeup I bought to wear at work contained nothing but red clay, aloe vera, and the like.

My obsession with everything natural provoked curiosity, and a mild contempt for that which is different, from the other dancers. As I sat at the bar eating broiled tofu and seaweed, I invariably attracted attention. "What's she eating today?" dancers would say. They'd gingerly finger the frayed edges of the old dresses I picked up at thrift shops to wear as costumes. They treated me as an oddity. "She's an artist," I overheard a woman saying, "a college girl." They were friendly enough to me, but there always existed a sense, on their part and mine, that I didn't quite belong there.

I wanted this differentness to make me seem less involved in "the life." Ironically, my pose required even more time and effort to keep up than the prescribed behavior for strippers took. While I did not spend hundreds of dollars on costumes, I did spend whole days traveling from thrift store to thrift store in search of costumes. I took as long to color my face with organic cosmetics as other dancers took with the synthetic variety. If other dancers could send the porter out for a slice of pizza, I had to peel, chop, and marinate my vegetables in advance. My "natural" approach in no way removed me from the Zone; it merely gave my involvement a different flavor.

At the same time, I wanted to be accepted by the other dancers. I didn't enjoy the deliberate silence that greeted my entrance into the dressing room. I wanted my attempts at conversation to be met with more than short and guarded responses.

I began to bring marijuana and caches of cocaine to work. I'd selectively invite dancers to join me in the bathroom to smoke a joint or "do a line." "I didn't know you got high," many of them confided. "You seem so straight." Thus I became less of an outsider. While I maintained my own style of eating and dressing, I did so less ostentatiously, giving those actions the minor emphasis they merited. Finally, I could participate in discussions about boyfriends, customers, and bosses, without being treated as a spy. Less to my advantage, I could be included in the rivalry over costumes, customers, and status.

I began to put up another defense. Capitalizing on the fact that I studied psychology at college, I became a "concerned listener." Empathetic yet not entangled, I tried to listen objectively and give advice. I thought of the dancers as "cases." The more I knew about them, the more valuable I'd be, and the more legitimacy I could add to my "participant-observer" role.

Sometimes I did believe that I stood apart from the other dancers as a kind of counselor, that my role as a student dominated my sense of self, and that I quite naturally stepped into that role at the Nudie-Tease. Then I'd remember that outside of work, at school, I identified with being a stripper.

My schooling included a training program in counseling. Often, I would work at the Nudie-Tease during the day. After eight hours of stripping, sweating, and in some ways functioning as a counselor in a much more vivid way than the classroom role plays could replicate, I would parade into a room of empathetic-looking people who were "giving support" to someone who was holding tension in his solar plexus because of a child

94

hood trauma. With makeup still smeared on my face, and sex and beer odors on my skin, I felt like I was still on stage. People's true feelings seemed no more real to me than my Lolita act.

I made it clear to the people in the training program that I lived a dual life. I was a student, yes, but I was also a stripper. How about that, folks? I'd say; can you still accept me now? If they could accept my stripping, I called them open-minded. If they couldn't, they fell into the general category of "up-tight."

At work, I was just one more stripper. So I took my clothes off. Didn't we all? So the men jeered, hollered, and whistled. Didn't they do that for everyone? I was not even one of the highly esteemed dancers. Outside of work, I became THE STRIPPER. I must be attractive if men would pay to look at me. I must possess the secret charm every woman yearned for. Outside of work, I could allow the illusions to filter back into my mind. Forgetting the smoke, catcalls, and groping fingers, I could recall the fantasy of the lights and the glitter. I could feel as sexy as the fantasy presumed me to be.

Like all the women at the Nudie-Tease, I put a wedge between myself and the other dancers, denied that we shared any common ground, and refused to look at the injury effected by the job.

Rebel protected herself by saying to all women, not just to lesbians, "Stay away!" Many of the dancers wanted to befriend her. They thought that if they positioned themselves close enough to one of the rising stars, some of her status might rub off on them. In a sense they were right; no one could spend time around Rebel without catching some of her enthusiasm for stripping. She believed that strutting up and down the runway at the Nudie-Tease, affixing her name out front in neon, and printing her name in the newspaper in an advertisement for the club would propel her into lasting fame. She felt so certain about this promised future that she spent all of her earnings, and spent them conspicuously. She drove to work every now and then in a rented Jaguar. She made the arrangements for her next Desiree in the dressing room, for all the dancers to hear. She bought the most chic gadgets with which to inhale her abundant supply of cocaine. With the cocaine in her system, she talked fast, and her energetic laugh echoed throughout the club. Her entrance into the dressing room could change apathy into a party spirit, and everyone wanted to be invited to her party.

Rebel wanted to hold the party at her convenience, and in celebration of herself. When she held the spotlight, she could tolerate her co-workers. When someone else commanded attention, or when she didn't feel like socializing, she pushed people away with a threatening silence or with insulting southern epithets. But even her most open invitations contained a deception; she did not really let anyone get close to her.

"I don't have any buddy buddies," she had told me. "I don't go through the trouble. As soon as you get close to a girl, you have a fight, and she's trying to get people on her side. Or else she gets fired and you never see her again. Or the next thing you know she's borrowing your lipstick; germs can spread that way. I was friends with this one girl. She ended up moving in with me. Turns out she had a drug habit real bad. She had somebody come in and rip off my TV and stereo, and then she left town. Never again."

"Don't you ever feel lonely at work?" I'd asked.

"*Me?* I can always talk to them, but only if I want to. I don't burden people with my problems and whine to them and stuff. That's a pain in the rear. I aim to have a good time with people."

"But where do you turn for support?"

"I turn to the mirror and talk to myself, or I talk to my mama. Why should I ask them crazy girls about something? If I can't figure it out, they sure can't. I don't have any close women friends."

96

"Rebel feels above those girls," her mother had told me, "and she is better. She's using the job instead of letting it use her."

While the banter went on about her night with Patrice, Charlene rushed into the dressing room. We all stopped talking. Her eyes were puffy and her hair hung limp around her face. Unlike most of us, who "put on our faces" at work, Charlene usually arrived at the Nudie-Tease with her hair swept up into a bun, her cheekbones accentuated with red, and her lips wet with lip gloss. While the rest of us smoothed skin-colored makeup over our faces to hide the imperfections in our complexions, she would sit in front of the mirror adding touches of powder to her already perfect camouflage. She gasped over a misplaced hair while we struggled to cover the dark circles under our eyes. Coming to work with her face already painted seemed a symptom of her overall docility. She was a stripper, the job defined her as such, and so she must present a stripper's face to the world at all times.

Today she must have forgotten that identity. She had a wild-eyed expression and wore no makeup on her face. Her usual uncanny resemblance to Marilyn Monroe, from the blond hair to the strategically placed beauty mark, had disappeared. In its place was a sad face with patchy skin, bloodshot eyes, and uncombed hair. Only her vague manner of moving and gesturing, which so many men at the Nudie-Tease characterized as alluring and insufferably feminine, remained the same.

"Girl, you better do something about that face." Rebel broke the silence. "Did a truck hit you?"

"I didn't have time," Charlene mumbled, trying to edge her way to her locker without being seen too clearly.

Rebel stepped in her path and stood only inches from Charlene, so that Charlene, uncomfortable with close contact with anyone or anything, tried to back away. "How was your night?" Rebel asked in a cloying tone.

The other dancers made no effort to suppress their laughter. Their gleeful faces reflected in the foreground of the mirror. Charlene's cringing posture formed the backdrop.

"Tell us about it," said Sugar. "How good is sisterhood?"

"Women!" Rebel shrieked, giving a poor imitation of Patrice's high voice. "Women loving women. What do you need men for when you've got *women?*"

Sugar pretended to gag. "Did it taste like fish? Did you get enough to eat?"

"Charlie came back." Charlene defended her heterosexuality. "He's sorry about leaving. It's okay now."

"Well, I declare, isn't that nice?" Rebel crooned. Each time Charlene backed away, Rebel stepped forward to regain her position; now the two of them stood against the wall. "Ya'll planning on getting married soon?"

"Soon," Charlene intoned.

"It better be soon, so you can use that dress. I'm ordering one next week. I'm the genuine southern belle around here."

Charlene winced, and then her eyes looked vacant. "You can be the star. You're the star, Rebel. I give up."

"Maybe a night with the girls put some sense in her head," Rebel said to us. She backed away from Charlene, looking a little guilty.

Charlene walked slowly to her locker. She wore an expensive woolen suit. The dark fabric, which clung tightly and curved over her breasts and hips, might have looked elegant any other day. Today it accentuated the almost transparent pallor of her skin, the circumspection of her movements, the ethereal way in which she avoided touching anything. As she undressed, I saw why she moved like an old woman. She had been beaten, and this time she had not covered her wounds. Her legs were mottled with blood seepage, and her belly had been scratched with some sharp object. Older bruises, starting to radiate out in yellow and black streaks, framed the compact and vivid marks of fresh blows.

Sugar and Tulip moved aside to make room for her at the makeup table. Charlene took the place they provided and began a noncommittal search through her cosmetic case for her rouge. Among the twenty or so tubes she deposited on the table, she could not find the color she wanted. Vaguely restive in her movements, she began to sort the tubes into piles, placing eyeshadow in one pile, lipstick in another. Watching her, I remembered the first time I'd met her at the Twilight Lounge, arranging straws in a similar fashion, to assure herself that Charlie would come to rescue her soon, and to give some shape to the nebulous period of waiting she had to endure. Again confronted with a situation over which she felt no control, she tried to impose order on the artifacts that helped her to contrive a particular identity. Without the proper makeup, she could not be a proper stripper, and if she were not a stripper, what would she be? Now she attempted a new arrangement, cataloging the tubes by color rather than by function. Still, she found no answer. She seemed utterly incapacitated by the dilemma of the missing rouge. She stared and stared at herself in the mirror.

"I give up," she said.

"Don't you ever say that," Rebel scolded, coming to stand behind Charlene; she was ready to defend the profession upon which she had staked her future. "You've got a lot going for you. You're a beautiful girl, one of Preston's favorites. You should count your blessings."

"You think so?" asked Charlene, a note of encouragement in her voice.

"Sure do. Most of the girls in here would mortgage their grandmothers to have one tenth of your good looks." Rebel embarked on a pep talk, carefully excluding herself from the ranks of envious dancers. She could afford to compliment Charlene now that Charlene's self-confidence had dipped to a depth too low to constitute a threat to Rebel's aspirations.

"I look like a ghost," Charlene whimpered, "like a nobody."

At that point, Rebel took over. With one sweep of her arm, she disrupted the neatness of Charlene's piles of makeup. She stationed herself between Charlene and the mirror, and boldly appraised Charlene's face. "What you need is a new image," she declared. "I'm going to make you over so nice you won't even know yourself."

Unresisting, Charlene allowed her face to be painted and her hair to be curled. She sat perfectly still, like a little girl at the hands of her mother, as Rebel twisted her hair into a bouncing array of banana curls, a style diametrically opposed to her customary Parisian knot. The hairstyle made her look like the fair daughter of an antebellum plantation owner. She looked lovely and pure, exempt from the turmoil of the society around her. We all sighed and applauded the miraculous transformation Rebel had effected. From the ruins of Charlene's Hollywood femme fatale, she had created a new and unbeaten woman.

The new woman eyed herself incredulously in the mirror. "Is that me?"

"It's the new you," Rebel said proudly. "I don't want to hear any more of that hogwash; I need some competition around here."

Even with her new appearance, Charlene would not be much competition. Although she seemed fairly convinced that Rebel had molded her into somebody beautiful, she did not seem any more comfortable with this new self than she had with the identities supplied to her by her mother, Red Hat, Preston, or Charlie. She still moved proscriptively, as if held by invisible reins, with no apparent volition of her own. And although she covered her bruises again, she must have been reminded of their existence each time she shifted her weight or touched any surface. She left the dressing room to begin her day's work.

Rebel proceeded to hold court in a corner of the dressing room with several dancers who wanted to sample her cocaine.

100

To subsidize her substantial habit, she had begun to sell the drug. She found an eager market among the dancers at the Nudie-Tease. With their salaries paid in cash, they felt rich enough on payday to spend one hundred dollars on a thimbleful of white powder.

Rebel never had to push her wares; people came to her. They knew how well cocaine complemented stripping. After inhaling two thin lines of it, they could perform their tired routines with fresh enthusiasm. In a cocaine-induced euphoria, they felt in their own bodies a ruminating promise of satisfaction like the never quite fulfilled promise that the sight of their bodies offered to the customers. The rhythm of the music was felt as a fluttering sensation in their bellies; their legs felt at once solid and fluid as they moved, propelled by the amphetamines cut into the pure cocaine. Their hearts raced. They breathed shallowly and savored the implosive tingling sensation created by the white powder as it descended from their nostrils to their throats. Soaring, their minds fixated on a time in the near future when all the hopes they created in their present state would come true: the dreams of fame, the resolution of all conflict, the body youthful, unchanging, and ideal, the feeling of netted-in safety in any environment, and most important, the assurance of more and more cocaine to keep and freeze and deter the destruction of this moment.

The illusions of omnipotence induced by the drug had their parallel in the elaborate ritual surrounding its preparation and inhalation. Rebel placed a tiny gold-topped vial of coke on the table. Next to it she laid a hand mirror, a plastic razor blade, and a container that looked like a miniature flour sifter with a crank on top of it. She tipped a few pearl-sized lumps of coke from the vial into the sifter, then turned the crank until the cocaine rained down onto the mirror in a fine powder. With the razor blade, she separated the powder into four slim lines across the glass.

"It's ninety-eight percent pure," she said, as she fashioned a straw out of a twenty dollar bill. "Colombian. Sweet, and no speed."

She gathered some of the frost left on the sifter on her finger, rubbed it on her gums, and offered some to Tulip. After anaesthetizing her gums, Tulip wet her fingers with ice water and inhaled the drops of water, to clear out her nostrils.

Finally, they took turns snorting the cocaine. Rebel held one nostril shut as she sucked up a line into her other nostril. Tulip did the same. After each inhalation, they threw their heads back, held their noses shut, and smiled.

"That's nice," said Tulip.

"Sweet as a baby," Rebel bragged.

In the opposite corner of the dressing room, Pandora sat crying. She rocked back and forth, hugging her thin legs to the solid mass of silicone that filled her breasts. We all assumed that she had become a woman through surgery. Her height, lean hips, and husky voice, coupled with her obsession with whether or not the men found her sufficiently feminine, did make our hunch seem plausible.

"He said I look like a man," she cried.

"One of our fine gentlemen told you that?" asked Rebel, as she accepted a wad of bills from Tulip, in exchange for a tiny envelope of cocaine.

"He said my ass didn't curve like a woman's," Pandora whined. She stood up to examine the curve of her buttocks in the mirror. "I'm skinny, that's all. Mine curves as much as Lolita's. Do they say that to you, Lolita?"

"No, I'd make an awfully short man."

"You sure would!" Rebel screamed. "That reminds me of this guy I met in here one time. He wanted to be my slave; handed me the chain to his dog collar. He was only like five foot four. Here I am towering over him. Sure! Why don't you go play in the freeway for a while? And you're going to call that a man?"

"Short people have feelings." I pouted in jest.

"I wouldn't know about that," Rebel retorted. "Right now I'm about as high as a Georgia pine. That's some good blow there."

Pandora wept still louder.

"You want some advice?" Rebel stood up to preach. "Listen up. You too, Lolita. All of ya'll that think your rear ends don't curve enough to get you a man. Remember that song, 'It Ain't the Meat, It's the Motion'? That's my words of wisdom."

"But I move good," Pandora protested.

"About as good as a dead pancake," said Rebel. "If you want them to like it, you've got to flaunt it. That's how to get a man."

"That's one method," I said.

"Speak up, then!" Rebel accepted my challenge. "Let's hear how Lolita gets her man."

I backed down. "I'm not talking about any particular method. I didn't read *How to Pick Up Guys* and memorize fifty come-ons guaranteed to be effective. I'm talking about getting to know a guy through conversation instead of being seen only for my body."

"That's baloney, and you know it." Rebel snorted at my self-righteous pose. "You want to know how to get a guy? You strut, honey. Shoot, yeah! And when you can't get him that way, you just walk right up and say, 'Hey you!' "

"That's bold, Rebel. I'm not that bold."

She went on, "Before I started stripping, I was like, Oh, what are people going to think? Now, if I feel like being crazy, I'm going to be crazy. I say what's on my mind, and I know how to get a guy. If he won't notice me, I'll go step on his foot."

"Is that how you met Skippy?"

"Skippy?" She looked at me like I was crazy. "He's long gone. My mama really put a boot up my butt about him. She kept saying, 'You're supporting Skippy out of your guilt complex, 'cause you figure you're making dirty money.' I knew she was right. I mean, she's my mama. I kicked the leech out, good enough. I do not cater to anyone now."

I thought of Virginia's portrayal of Rebel as a sweet, kittenish little girl. In one sense, Rebel's construction of femininity did have that childlike quality. For all her boldness, she dressed only in pastel-colored costumes. She wore so much perfume and powder that her body served as a roving stick of incense. Adult bodily secretions such as sweat and menstrual blood disgusted her. Playful and optimistic, she seemed untarnished by the gloom around her.

Beyond doing the work, she did it passionately. She believed in the image of the stripper as the ultimate good girl, the untouchable icon of a woman-worshiping society. She did this, I thought, by polarizing the different parts of herself. Just as she could do a floor show with her hand strategically placed, she could strategically place a rigid boundary between her soft interior and her bold exterior. She needed both parts of herself. She knew, from her childhood, that she had to fight for what she wanted, but part of what she fought for was a chance to be as vulnerable, ladylike, and protected as the myths of the show girl, girl child, and southern lady said she would be. She used her toughness to keep at bay anything that threatened her "femininity." She pushed for stardom, thinking that the club owners would become her protectors if they valued her enough; then they'd fend off danger in the worldly sphere of competition and violence, while she retreated to the womanly world of beauty, piety, and high moral standards. But she had difficulty preserving her "true nature," as Virginia put it, because the very attributes of the childlike lady—idleness, naïveté, openness—were by necessity excluded from the reality of the working woman.

Rebel found a stopgap solution to her dilemma in cocaine. It simultaneously numbed and inspired her. It helped her to become strong enough to fend off the strip joint's viperous threats to her innocence, while it also helped her to infuse that ideal of pure womanhood with more and more potency. Cocaine froze in bold relief two ostensibly contradictory strands of self-image.

"Who's your old man?" Rebel asked me. "Is that the dude who picks you up after work?"

"That's him. His name is Lamont."

"He's been around almost a year, if I recall correctly. Ya'll fixing to get married?"

"He's not too anxious to try that out again," I explained. "But that's fine with me. I'm only twenty. No hurry."

"You sure he's not a leech?" Rebel asked.

"He's got a job. He's a substitute teacher." After some thought, I admitted, "When we're out to have a good time, I'm the one paying."

"Ain't it the truth? Those men just love us strippers with our carefree money."

"I can't seem to hold on to any of it. I pay my bills, and then what's left I spend, because I know I can make it up in drinks the next day."

"It's the most slippery dang stuff," Rebel agreed.

"After working here all day, I want to treat myself to something nice. Lamont and I go out to dinner, and I pay. It's a way of paying him for coming down here to get me. Protection."

"You've got the makings of a leech on your hands," Rebel warned me. "First you're taking him to dinner, and the next thing you know, you're stuffing his nose with blow."

"No way. It's not about that." I felt that Rebel vulgarized the love between Lamont and me.

She ignored my protest. "And I bet he's jealous about who you're sitting with at the club and what you're doing. You can't tell him enough that you're not doing anything but dancing and joining gentlemen for drinks, can you?"

"Wrong again. He trusts me. If I tell him what I do, it's because I need to tell someone. He never pries."

"You wait and see," Rebel said ominously. "He'll come around."

Rebel's allegations contained a piece of truth. In the year that I'd known Lamont, I'd seen him use his anger in two ways. He could join me in blasting my bosses and customers, or he could turn his anger on me. His temper would flare up unexpectedly, and I'd do anything to pacify him. As he worked fewer and fewer days substitute teaching, I began to subsidize him. While I told myself that I gave him money to help him through a tight time, I knew that the money induced him to be kinder to me. But I couldn't expect him to be perfect; I wasn't. He loved me, and that was what counted.

Vita poked her head in the dressing-room door to yell at us. "You can't hang in here all day," she hollered. "Get out there and mix. Lolita, Shakespeare's waiting for you."

"Shit. The money's not worth the abuse he dishes out."

"You want your job?"

"I don't mix before my first show," Rebel announced. "And you better watch your tone, Vita." As Vita shut the door, Rebel called out to her, "Hold it. I got to ask you something."

"I have got work to do," Vita said tensely. "I'm supposed to tell these young ladies when their shows are. You think I have time to sit around like you?"

"That's what I want to ask you. What's a pretty girl like you hiding up there with the records for, when you could be making good money like the rest of us?"

"You really want me to answer that?" asked Vita, stepping into the dressing room and shutting the door behind her.

"I do," Rebel nodded. "I can't understand why a girl would come to this pit to spin records for peanuts instead of dancing. You don't get any recognition or money, and there's no future in what you're doing."

"That's your first mistake right there," Vita interrupted. "It's dancing that's got no future. If you're upset that I get

106

flowers without having to take anything off, you better look at your own guilt."

"What guilt?" Rebel snorted. "I'm so clean I can have my mama watch me."

"About your second point," Vita continued, "I have no fantasies about being up on stage. If there's one thing I've never had a problem with it's being noticed by men. In college I had a trail of them like a damn pack of dogs after me. I thought, Is there something wrong with me? Do I look funny? Why do all these men want to go to bed with me? Sex, at that time, did not feel good to me. I couldn't understand why people praised it so highly."

"You'll fit right in, then." Rebel twisted Vita's words. "Most of us don't like sex. Isn't that right, Lolita?"

"I probably know more about what's going on in this place than anyone in here." Vita's voice dropped almost to a whisper. "I talk to a lot of the dancers about their problems. Maybe because I'm older, I know their anxieties. Sure, they're doing it for the money. In the beginning they do dig the lights, the attention. After a while it gets to them. They say, Damn, I want to be respected for who I am. My real name isn't Genevieve, it's Jill. I am a person. The management does not regard the dancers as people. Dancers to them are machines. I don't care if you're the star or the lowest one on the totem pole."

"That's a lie," Rebel mumbled.

"All I'm saying is that I don't put my faith in anyone but me. This job is a chance to get some ground-floor experience in DJ'ing, and nothing else. I'm trying to get into a radio station, and that's hard in this city unless you know someone. I am very persistent. People say, Let's just hear this woman to get her out of our hair. Someday I'm going to get the job I want. Meanwhile, I'm not going to let anyone walk over me."

Vita checked her watch. Realizing that she had only two minutes left to set up the records for the next dancer's set, she flew out of the dressing room.

Rebel turned to the mirror to check her makeup one last time before going out on the floor. "I'm going to have to get Vita cross more often. The only exercise she gets is running off at the mouth."

"And running after us to get us on stage on time," I added.

"Didn't she look cute standing there with her hands on her hips like that? I declare, she ought to be on the stage."

SIX

THE PLEASURE
OF YOUR COMPANY

When the old man came into the bar alone, early in 1980, I couldn't quite place him. Six months earlier, he had brought his wife with him. They had sat in a booth sipping orange juice, his attention fixed on the woman on stage, his wife's on him. The old woman had still seemed like an Italian peasant, with her rough-sewn clothes and halting English. Her face had looked pained, and I'd thought the pain grew out of this new form of submission to the rule of her husband, this viewing of strippers. His expression, in comparison, had been beatific; at last he had seen a naked female body.

Now, six months later, he walked into the club wearing a cheap American suit, and asked to see me. As I approached him, wondering how this old man who wore a starched handkerchief in his breast pocket and doused himself with so much cologne that I could smell him ten feet away, knew my name, I recalled the earlier scene.

"Where's your wife?" I asked straight off.

"Gone." He brushed his hand through the air.

"Back to Italy?"

"My wife was a sick woman," he said euphemistically. After a short silence, he motioned to me, "Sit. I want to buy a drink. That's what they do here, no?"

"It costs seven dollars," I told him.

"I can pay," he assured me, patting his pocket. He ordered a soda, no liquor, for me, and a beer for himself.

"Why no liquor?" I asked.

"No good," he explained. "You're young."

I felt a sudden desire to cover my breasts around this man who acted like a father. "I don't even remember your name," I confessed.

"John."

"That wasn't your name. You had an Italian name."

"Forget Italian. John is my new name."

He spoke with pride about the new contours of his life. After his wife died, he'd left the close-knit North End of Boston to live with his eldest son in a sparkling new suburb. They had a new washer and dryer there, in a separate room. Each of the grandsons had his own room, and they even had a finished cellar for the kids to play in. His daughter-in-law drove a late-model American car to the shopping mall to do her errands, and she was a beautiful girl with blond hair. Just recently, she'd signed up to work with the Catholic charities one afternoon a week in the city. To give John a change of pace, she brought him along and dropped him off in the department store district to window-shop, have a cup of coffee, and watch the passersby. As soon as she disappeared, he quickly walked over two blocks to the Combat Zone.

After that day, he returned to the Nudie-Tease every Tuesday for the next six months. Knowing that I could expect him promptly at two o'clock, I tried to be free to sit with him at that hour. In terms of money, he made a poor customer. I sat with him for an hour; he bought me one drink right away, and another after a half hour, each time counting out his money carefully and gallantly leaving the waitress a dime. But as a

110

companion, he started out as the nicest customer I'd ever had.

Shyly at first, and later more boldly, John courted me. Each week, he brought a gift, some small trinket. Once he brought me a pair of dime-store earrings that were so cheap that they turned my ears green. On Valentine's Day, he gave me a box of chocolates; on Easter, a plastic painted egg. I accepted a tiny crucifix from him, not having the heart to tell him that I wasn't Christian. He wrapped these gifts in tissue paper and tied them with ribbon. I'd playfully try to guess the contents of the package while he looked on.

"It's a candle," I ventured when he handed me a long slim box.

"Not a candle," he said.

"Then it's a sausage."

"No, no. Open it."

It was a Barbie doll, dressed in a miniskirt, and outfitted with an extra change of clothes.

"You like it?"

I kissed him on the cheek. As a child, I'd wanted a Barbie doll. My mother forbade it, saying that no woman had legs twice as long as her torso and breasts that pointed out like twin icicles. "I love it."

If John caught cold, I worried about him. I scolded him for going out in the winter without a hat. He, in turn, chided me about my weight, telling me that I'd waste away unless I ate more than vegetables. At one point, he sneaked portions of his daughter-in-law's pastries out of the house to bring me. Later, he tried to give me money to buy a hamburger.

After a few months, John's concern for me began to take on a sexual tone. Perhaps he realized that his new life not only gave him the freedom to see naked women, but that it put within his reach their sexual services. Yet he never tried to touch me. Verbal allusions to sex, and its symbolic presence all around him in the Nudie-Tease, seemed to satisfy him. He didn't want sexual relief; he wanted to prove to himself that as an American man, he could have anything he wanted.

The gifts changed. He brought me silk stockings, lacy underwear, and cheap perfume. He became curious about my love life. Did I have many boyfriends? Did I let them do it to me from behind? Did I like sex? I tried to shift the conversation back to earlier topics.

"Tell me again about your farm in Italy," I urged him.

Instead, he'd talk about sex with his wife, and as if she were still alive. "She acts like she doesn't want it, but it was good. She liked it." He finished his beer. "You know how she says?"

"No, don't tell me."

He moaned in imitation of his wife, and laughed at me when I covered my ears.

Instead of staying at the Nudie-Tease for one hour, he stayed until fifteen minutes before the Catholic charities closed; then he'd rush to meet his daughter-in-law. His drinking had gotten heavier, and I wondered how he concealed his afternoon activities from her. Once he showed up on a Friday, saying that no woman could control where he went, and when; he'd taken the train into town.

Whereas at first he bought one beer and didn't even drink it, he gradually worked his way up to seven or eight. He left the bar quite drunk. He also began to insist that I drink real drinks. I didn't, and he never knew the difference, but I felt that I'd lost a friend, who took a genuine interest in my well-being, to the hustle at the Nudie-Tease. He began to act like scores of other men, young and old, who came to the bar. He now whistled at me on stage and sat close when I did a floor show. He whispered obscenities to me when I sat with him, and shouted them at me when I danced. With bravado, he turned to the men around him to state what he'd do with that girl on stage if he got her in bed.

Occasionally, when he'd drunk beyond his capacity for alcohol, he'd begin to reminisce. In slurred English and Italian, he'd talk about people he'd known and situations he'd been in

112

during his lifetime. The seven and a half decades of his life merged, so that he'd talk about someone he'd known fifty years ago and someone he'd met a week ago as though they existed in the same milieu, or talk about the dead as if they were still living. He transposed incidents from his childhood to the United States, and imposed his boyhood identity on his grandsons. None of it made much sense, logically, but taken as a whole, his drunken ravings formed a montage in which all the loves and hatreds of his life coalesced.

Invariably, he'd resurrect his wife during these episodes. "She's a beautiful girl, and I tell her father I want to marry her. The big eyes, and I tell her, It won't hurt, no pain. I seen her dance. I am the man. Catholic charities. Don't tell me be at the corner at five o'clock. I'm the man. Pussy. Cunt. They cut off her foot before she died. My wife, she's a good woman. I love her. I go to Switzerland; they tell me Italians work for dirt. I tell her, My only daughter can't go to America, and she goes. I like the titties. Maria, I love your pretty hands. Marry me."

If he cried, I held his hand and waited until he finished. Sometimes I felt guilty, as if I'd enticed him into the Combat Zone and encouraged him to return week after week. Other times, I thought it must do him good, this catharsis. When I couldn't stand to hear any more of his life torn into fragments, I'd remove myself by thinking, Isn't this interesting; I ought to present this case to my class.

No matter how much he drank and how far into his memories he traveled, John managed to leave the club in time to meet his daughter-in-law. He'd return to the Zone the next Tuesday.

Most of the dancers had at least one regular customer. We coveted these men because they made our workday easier. Instead of walking around the bar asking man after man to buy us drinks, we could relax with one man we knew. Even if he had a foot fetish or drank until he passed out, we knew what to expect and learned to cope with him. Many of these relationships had a romantic quality to them, if only on the man's part. Occasionally, a dancer would reciprocate, and a full-fledged affair would develop. More often than not, dancers would keep these love affairs in the club and milk the men for champagne, gifts, and flowers.

Charlene had a regular customer named Eddie. I never knew exactly what he did for a living; it had something to do with gambling. He carried around huge wads of cash, yet spent most of his time at the Nudie-Tease. Every few months he'd disappear for a week, and then return, acting as if nothing had happened. In his early thirties, and handsome in a clean-cut way, he surely could have found a woman outside of the Nudie-Tease. Perhaps he did have a wife at home, a whole other life none of us knew about. Or perhaps he wanted a woman whom he could never actually touch. He may have thrived off the illusion that he could save Charlene, a lost soul, from her demise in the Combat Zone. Whatever his motivation, one thing was clear: He adored Charlene.

He sat with her for hours at a time. If she wanted champagne, he bought her champagne. If she wanted to sit with someone else, he waited for her. He applauded her dancing, even when she weaved drunkenly across the stage. He had two dozen roses delivered to the dressing room, with the inscription, "I'll love you forever." The value of the gifts he lavished on her added up to a small fortune: a fur coat, a diamond ring, a full wardrobe of clothing.

As her drinking increased, he tried to help her to curb it. He offered to send her to an expensive program to dry out; she refused. Not aware that she kept a stash of whiskey in her locker, he asked the bartenders to leave the liquor out of her drinks. He'd bring her coffee from the pizza place next door. At lunchtime, he'd walk over several blocks and bring her back a four-course meal.

Sitting next to them at the bar, I'd sometimes overhear their conversations. Eddie knew about Charlie. As long as Charlie

114

made Charlene happy, Eddie didn't mind that she lived with another man. He didn't make the connection between Charlie and her bruises. She told him she fell down a lot; he told her she shouldn't drink so much. And he idolized her body. She should protect it and keep it lovely, soft, and perfect, he'd say. She never responded to his attentions, neither the gifts nor the compliments. When Eddie disappeared for a week, she sat with other customers. When he returned, she went back to him, as if by habit, as if it made little difference to her where she sat. He continued to court her, seemingly content with their level of involvement, for over two years.

Most of our regulars had time constraints and limited supplies of money. If Charlene could spend the entire afternoon with Eddie, we had to get out on the floor and hustle. Hustling meant something different at the Nudie-Tease than it had meant at the Twilight Lounge. We had no official quota of drinks to earn in a day. The management enforced an unofficial quota, hovering between ten and twenty drinks a day, by using positive reinforcement in the form of compliments and pay raises, and negative reinforcement in the form of warnings and refusals to grant pay increases. Because we never knew the precise acceptable minimum, we devised a relative scale based on how many drinks other dancers were getting that day. Throughout the day, we asked each other the loaded question, "How many drinks do you have?" Competition for drinks became fierce at times. Being a "good mixer" meant gaining status and greater job security, as well as earning extra money.

Preston spoke of mixing as our duty to the club. We had to earn our keep, he'd say. In his view, mixing, not dancing, made up the real substance of our work. We danced to lure men into the club so that we could then persuade them to buy drinks. By this reasoning, dancing became a gratuitous act that we did to puff up our egos enough to withstand the toil of mixing. That made no sense to me. Dancing was hard work, and men paid to see it. They willingly paid two dollars and seventy-five cents for a domestic beer they could buy for a dollar twenty-five at any other bar, just to watch us perform. When we sold drinks on top of that, we added even more to the club's earnings. Somehow, I couldn't accept the loyalist attitude of many of the dancers, who believed that their efforts at mixing kept the bar afloat, and who felt too proud to accept "charity" for dancing.

As "clean mixers," we had to try harder to convince men to buy drinks for us. We couldn't stroke a man's thighs and tell him we'd make good company, as dancers did in other clubs. We had a classy image to uphold. Preston wanted us to hustle without seeming like we were hustling. While presenting a polite and cultured exterior, we were supposed to entice a man into spending all of his money. This should be done with such cunning that the man would never realize that the woman at his side had mercenary, not romantic, intentions. We had to learn the proper measure of assertiveness to get the drink without scaring the guy off.

Dancers had unique methods of hustling. Some women walked around the bar asking every single man if he'd like company, until they found a man who would buy. Others approached the procedure more scientifically; they divided the men into categories and only approached those categories that had statistically proven to be profitable. Some dancers stayed with a man for half an hour, hoping he'd buy them a second drink. Others restricted their conversations, refusing to sit for longer than ten minutes per drink. Shanti, an art student, would draw a portrait of a man on a bar napkin, using it as an entry into a conversation. Adele flattered the customers. "That's a beautiful tie," she'd say. "Did you select it? Did your wife select it?" Each speck of information she could garner from the man's response she'd use to build a dialogue. Rebel walked up to men she'd never seen before and said, "Where've you been all this time? I've missed you." Startled, many of these men bought her drinks.

I found it easiest to get drinks right after I finished dancing.

Sometimes, men asked me to join them after my performance. Usually, however, I harnessed my vigor from dancing and made my way around the bar in search of a "spender." Some men agreed to drink with me in order to find out why my eyes glazed over and my lips twisted into a detached and crooked smile while I danced. Others didn't recognize me although I'd danced right in front of them minutes before. Depending on my luck, I could land a drink immediately, or I could approach every man in the bar with no success.

To be an aggressive mixer, a dancer had to believe that a man ought to spend seven dollars to talk to her for a few minutes. She had to believe in the mystique of the stage, which gave her the glamour of a movie star and made the men into groveling autograph seekers. She had to accept the model of courtship in which the man wooed the woman by spending money on her. I didn't believe any of that. Essentially, I thought of the seven-dollar drinks as a waste of money. I imagined that many of the men felt foolish for spending their money that way, especially if they realized that the drinks didn't contain alcohol. Many customers responded angrily to me. They'd come to the club to immerse themselves in the belief system I scorned, and I denied them that pleasure. I considered them fools for needing to come to a strip joint and buy seven-dollar drinks.

I tried to take rejection in stride. When I first started dancing, I cried for an hour in the dressing room after being turned down by every man in the bar. Each refusal felt like a slap. After a few weeks, I began to see that dozens of factors influenced a man's decision to buy or not to buy. The weather, the state of the economy, a man's preference for tall women, his bewitchment with another dancer's little toe, or any number of odd causes could determine his response. I couldn't take it personally, I reasoned, because it had very little to do with me.

Still, after two years at the Nudie-Tease, I felt wounded

when a man spewed his pent-up rage out at me because I'd asked him for a drink. "Ugly cunt," he growled, "get lost." I retreated, feeling that I must learn to protect myself better. Up to that point, I'd thought of the dangers in the Zone in physical terms: I could get knifed or raped on my way home. Right then, I perceived the psychological danger. An illusion of intimacy accompanied nakedness. It was as if, by taking my clothes off in front of men, the customers and employers, I could expect them to know me and care for me. I trusted that intimates would understand my humanness, my moods and predicaments. I believed, still, in the magic of my sexual attractiveness. I'd grown up to believe in my body as the prize with which to reward men for their protection, love, and devotion to me. How could these men who had seen my most private parts not cherish me?

This was when I began to try, on a more conscious level, to separate Lolita and all her feelings from me. I kept a separate diary for her. I referred to her in the third person. To men who insisted, "That's not your real name," I maintained that I'd been born with none other. I increased my trips to the bathroom to get high until I spent all of my working hours stoned on marijuana, cocaine, or both. If I reached a point of emotional exhaustion, I hid out in the bathroom until I'd garnered the strength to face the men without feeling vulnerable to their judgments of me. Sometimes I spent half the day in hiding, coming out only to dance my shows.

Not all my encounters with customers were abusive or even terribly interesting. Most of them were as unremarkable as any conversation with a man in a bar. Because the men had already seen me nude, they tended to talk about sex and to proposition me more readily than they might have done elsewhere. I heard the same lines over and over again: "What's a nice girl like you doing in a place like this?" "Do you get turned on when you dance?" "You should be ashamed." "I bet you're good in bed." "Strippers are low-class sleazy women." "If my girlfriend did it, I'd beat the shit out of her." "You're the most beautiful girl I ever saw. Will you go to bed with me?" "How much do you cost?" Unless a man absolutely demanded my full attention, or broached a compelling topic, I'd tune out. Every few minutes I'd interject a question, to keep the man occupied with a response. I'd nod my head, and say mmhmmm, and not hear a word.

Pimps had a knack for spotting women who had tuned out. An alert woman would suspect a rap that began, "You're not making enough money at this job. I know of something easier that could win you five times as much." She'd either walk away from him, because she thought of pimps as scum, or she'd tell him he could buy her drinks if he wanted to, but that he'd get nowhere with her. If a dancer who had taken too many drugs, or who felt bad about herself, encountered a pimp, she'd be less likely to discern the self-serving motives beneath his flattery and grandiose job offers.

Sugar told me about the time she almost "blew it" with a pimp named Lucky. "He came on slick, but he didn't look like the slick type. He was real tall and had these big eyes. I was kind of down, and he'd come in telling me I was beautiful, I was his woman, he could make me happy. He turned me on to some blow, and bought me drinks. But he'd never watch me on stage. The first time I met him, he said, 'I'll check you out and I'll tell you the truth about what I think about you up there.' I was nervous I'd do a bad job and he'd leave. I was shaking. When I got off stage, I asked him what he thought. He said, 'You were beautiful, baby. I looked at you once. That's it.' He had me after that. It was like I had to try to get him to turn on to me. He was acting cool, keeping me hanging on. I was ready to do anything for him. I was ready to beg him to pimp me. I snapped out of it, but it was close. He was real smooth."

Preston tried to keep pimps out of the club. He didn't want them coming in and stealing "his girls." Just as pimps could profit from our bodies, so could Preston. And just as dancers refuted any similarities between themselves and prostitutes, Preston denied that he functioned as a pimp. Yet he wanted all of the money we teased out of the customers' pockets to go directly into the till; at the end of the day, after he had taken his ample cut, we could collect our pittance. He offered us the same service pimps ostensibly offered hookers: protection from other pimps and protection from the law.

The pimps who flaunted their hats and gold and cocaine never made it past the doorway at the Nudie-Tease; Victor booted them out. The men who were serious enough about pimping to do it without a show squeezed past the bouncers. For weeks at a time, a pimp might try to seduce a targeted dancer into his way of life. Occasionally, he'd make a conquest. I'd see a dancer in the dressing room one day and spot her out on the street soon after. Most pimps didn't get that far with their recruiting efforts. Someone would uncover their intent and they'd be ousted.

With the pimps gone, the dancers could turn to the valued customers, the men who bought drinks not to convince the women to leave their jobs, but to convince them to stay. These men spanned every social class, marital status, nationality, age, and occupation. I sat with construction workers, doctors, truck drivers, con artists, a congressman, a world-class boxer, college professors, street bums, prisoners on furlough, army recruits on leave, therapists, a priest, machine operators, and many others. If they had money, and if they comported themselves properly, the Nudie-Tease professed to welcome them. In fact, white men with money received the warmest welcome.

When Shakespeare walked through the door, the staff leaped to his service. He'd been a steady and generous customer for years. He'd hand his charge card to the waitress before he sat down, and wouldn't bother to ask the total cost of the champagne and drinks he'd bought before he left. He'd sing and recite sonnets and, granted, take up an inordinate amount of the bar help's time, but they considered him worth the trouble. "Lolita!" They'd fetch me from wherever I sat. "Shakespeare's here." I had no choice but to join him immediately, even if I had to leave another customer abruptly. Shakespeare had to be pleased and appeased; he represented a lot of money.

From the stage, I saw him enter the bar in mid-afternoon about a week after I'd met him, in 1977. Shadowed in the entrance of the Bare Beaver Bar, his bulk and height diminished by poor posture, he waited like a patron at a posh dinner spot to be seated. Delighted to see him, I waved enthusiastically. He ignored me. Two minutes later, the waitress left a note for me by the side of the stage. It read, "Flagrant displays of recognition do not become one of your stature. Never wave. Come see me when you put your clothes back on."

Upon reading the note, I felt the first tinges of the confusion that was to imbue my entire relationship with Shakespeare. What did he mean by "one of your stature"? I wondered. Did he refer to my height, my profession, or my status within my profession? Did he mean to reprimand me, tease me, or flatter me by saying that I had too much class to resort to indiscretions? I felt at once thankful that he wanted to see me, and ashamed, as if I'd done something wrong. To his stature as a man with money, position, age, and literary wealth far beyond my own, I attached his right to determine the tone and structure of our interactions.

When I joined him after my set, he bombarded me with charm. He stood up to greet me and kissed my hand. "May I have the pleasure of your company?" he asked.

He motioned for me to sit on the inside of the booth, nearer to the wall. Knowing that house rules required the dancers to sit on the outside of the booths, for our own protection against customers who tried to force our hands to their groins, or theirs to ours, I declined. You first, I motioned.

"I could take that as an affront," Shakespeare frowned.

"However, I see it as a sign of your ignorance. Now sit down where I told you."

I stalled, torn between the wish to comply with the club's rules and the desire to curry the favor of this obviously valuable customer. I also wondered, if I decided to defy Shakespeare's order, on what grounds I'd do that. Would I defer to the power of the club's behavior code? The management discouraged that; they wanted to mystify their control by filtering it through the illusion of an omnipotent feminine spell cast over all the doings in the club. They wanted us to obey all their rules, but to convince the customers that we followed only our womanly wiles. I couldn't imagine doing that with Shakespeare. His potency, inside and outside the club, as a wealthy, older, and educated man, dwarfed my little force of flirtations and seductions.

"What's the problem here?" the waitress hissed at me.

I explained my dilemma.

"Are you crazy?" she fairly exploded. "He's the boss. Do whatever he wants."

So we sat, with me against the wall, and Shakespeare on the open edge of the seat, where he could signal the waitress when he wanted her and appraise the shapes of the dancers as they walked by.

He told me about his three daughters. "The youngest one is going to be twenty-five next week, and I'm going to give her the biggest party you've ever seen. Caviar, champagne. Nothing too good for my baby. She understands me. I've brought her here. Everyone asked me, 'Where'd you find that gorgeous dame?' And I told them, 'She's my baby.' She was the tallest, best-looking one in here."

"What's this about height?" I asked.

"You know, I've been around the world ten times. I've vacationed in a modern-day harem with one hundred odalisques. I've been bathed by geishas. In India, I bought ten luscious virgins for the price of a steak. There's only one thing I've never done; I've never been with a short girl."

"You've never been attracted to a short woman?"

"They're ridiculous. Imagine if I took you to bed. Your nose would come to my navel, and my you-know-what would stab you in the chest." He laughed uproariously at the picture he'd painted. "I might try it some time."

I pictured him in the room of the hotel where he'd probably bring me to have sex. He'd emerge from the bathroom in a silk robe he'd picked up in Hong Kong. With his wig neatly brushed and his eyes tearing as always, he'd kneel by the bed to recite a love poem. Then he'd rub his arthritic hands over my body and tell me how little of me there was. Every few minutes, he'd cough up a wad of phlegm into the spittoon by the bedside. Enough, I thought. Let me desexualize this conversation while I can.

"What inspired you to memorize so much Shakespeare?" I asked.

"As an actor in the drama of life, I should know my lines. 'All the world's a stage.' "

" 'And all the men and women merely players,' " I concluded. Even I knew that passage.

"Very good," Shakespeare said sourly. "And what's the next line?"

"I have no idea. I know about three lines of Shakespeare, total."

"Then if you're smart, you'll shut up."

Again, I felt confused. I added up the contradictions he'd presented that day. He seemed glad to see me, yet he scolded me for greeting him with pleasure. He found short women "ridiculous," yet he chose me, at five feet three quarters of an inch, from among a dozen taller women at the Nudie-Tease. He said he liked smart women, yet he silenced me when I tried to join him in literary repartee.

123

Over the next two years, I grew to understand the rules of the game he wanted to play. He was a seriously ill man who knew that he'd die within a few years. "Death is the only person I can't buy off," he told me. "I wish I could." From this position of final impotence, he asserted his potency wherever he could. In a strip joint, he could buy illusions of power. He could claim to be youthful by hiding in the dim lights, by buying people off with drinks and tips in exchange for their inattention to his aging appearance and ill health, and by purchasing the company of young women, whose presence vindicated his claims to continued virility. An unarticulated fury underlined these claims. It enraged him to think that he, a man who had bought whatever he fancied with cash, wit, and influence, should now be so degraded as to need such a subterfuge. And he projected that degradation onto me. As he'd been cut down, he intended to belittle me.

First he'd build me up, comparing me to porcelain dolls he'd seen in the Far East. Just as I began to bask in his praise, he'd startle me with a flurry of slurs on short people. He'd insist that he wanted my company, but then he'd invite several other women to join us, always the tallest ones working that day. While they listened disinterestedly, he'd tell them how short and inadequate I was. After making a show of treating me like a lady, by kissing my hand and pulling out my chair for me, he'd fondle my knee under the table, to show me that in fact I was a whore. He wanted me to be intelligent so that when he uncovered my stupidity he'd have proven something significant.

At times I despised him, and at other times I pitied him. Each time he coughed, I'd think, These are his final wishes; they may as well be granted. And for all of his offensive qualities, he had a flair about him. I thrilled to his tales of adventure in foreign countries. I got my first real exposure to Shakespearean sonnets through him. I could best handle him, I learned, by giving him the stage. In that way, I'd extend the calm between his rages.

He stopped buying drinks for me eventually, replacing me with a pretty, eighteen-year-old neophyte. I wondered on what basis he'd put her down.

I felt that I could have only one revenge in the Combat Zone: I could be ruthless in my drink hustling. Although that defense would have little meaning to a rich man like Shakespeare, it would hurt most of our customers. But I didn't want my anger to fill up the cash registers. I also felt sorry for many of the men.

Sometimes I sat with John to protect him from the hard-hitting hustlers. With his heavy drinking, he'd lost much of his attachment to me, and would as gladly have sat with any other woman. I felt guilty, as if I'd encouraged him to return to the club each week, knowing that each visit destroyed him a bit more. I'd married myself to him, emotionally. I'd been with him when he saw his first naked female body; I'd witnessed his decay; now I felt obligated to nurse him through this wan period of drunkenness.

He became quite unruly at times, shouting out lewd phrases to the dancers on stage and trying to involve the men around him in his intoxicated conviviality. He even began to goose dancers as they walked by him.

"Don't do that," I warned him.

"I paid my money," he drawled.

Finally, the inevitable happened; he touched the wrong woman. Rebel turned on him with such fury that he cowered.

"Get your scummy hands off my body!" she screeched. "You I-talian swine."

John hung his head in shame. I didn't know if he regretted grabbing her or if he felt stung by the reminder that he was not an American. He raked his hands through his hair, from nape to forehead, leaving gray tufts standing upright and messy. Covering his face with his hands, he rocked his scraggy frame back and forth on the barstool.

I didn't see Victor approach. I saw two thick hands grab John's neck and slam his head down onto the bar. These hands lifted him by the collar and dragged him off his barstool. I saw his face, unconscious and aged, his nose bleeding slightly and his mouth agape, as Victor deposited him outside the front door of the Nudie-Tease.

Lamont picked me up from work that day.

"How was your day?" he asked.

"Fine. I got twenty drinks."

"Who'd you sit with?"

"I don't remember. No one impressive."

"Did anyone proposition you?"

"No."

We went through this ritual every day I worked. We both knew that I lied. Of course I'd been propositioned, and I remembered at least some of the men I'd sat with. There was something in the repetition of questions and answers that helped each of us put some closure on my workday. It worked only superficially. The effects of my stripping tainted our entire relationship.

We went to dinner at an Italian restaurant in the North End of Boston. While we waited for our meal, we sipped red wine. It tasted bitter, and I wondered why we'd chosen an Italian restaurant. It reminded me of John. What had his real name been? What had his life been like, in the hills of northern Italy? I remembered the resigned expression on his wife's face when I'd met her. And then I flashed on the blood on John's lip and the unconscious bobbing of his head as Victor dragged him across the floor.

"What are you thinking about, love?" asked Lamont.

He seemed far away, and I wanted to keep him at a distance.

126

He wouldn't understand my love for an old man I'd met in the Combat Zone. He'd see it as infidelity, when it had nothing to do with him.

"Nothing," I answered. "Just spacing out."

"No you weren't," he said. "You were thinking about Jack."

As always, he brought up my past lovers. My job, the real source of tension between us, remained unmentioned during these cross-examinations, while Lamont invented romances between me and all my former boyfriends. I had, in fact, been faithful to him in the two years I'd known him, finding monogamy a relief after several years of determined promiscuity. He knew that. But to tackle the real problem, to question why I worked as a stripper and why he condoned my work even as he felt torn by jealousy and worry about my safety, raised too many risks. We both depended on my job for the money to live our frivolous life-style and for a sense of righteous struggle in the face of overwhelming odds.

I knew why he avoided talking about the job, and yet I still felt attacked when he accused me of desiring Jack. My stomach began to churn. I wanted to reach out and slap him across the face. He looked hideous with his eyes narrowed into angry slits and his lips drawn back fiercely against his teeth. I hated him.

But I loved this man. I couldn't afford to hate him. If he left me, I'd be alone. I needed a man to come home to after stripping all day. I needed him. I had to calm him before he abandoned me.

I reached out across the table to squeeze his hand. "I could make love to you all night," I whispered in conciliation. And then my apology, "It's the job. It gets to me sometimes. Forgive?"

"I do. There's a lot to fight against in that place. I'm with you all the way, babe." He thrust out his chin, and I knew that we were partners in struggle again. He accepted my plea for intimacy. "I'll help you forget it. My house?"

I paid the bill and we left the restaurant.

With Lamont's head on my shoulder, we lay quietly at dawn. He snored softly, and, soothed by the rhythm of his breath, I drifted into sleep.

I never saw John again.

SEVEN

THE GIRLS
ARE NOT EXPLOITED

When I returned to the Nudie-Tease from a two-week vacation, I saw a sign posted in the dressing room. It said, "Contest: the most creative dancer will receive a free videotape session." It struck me as odd that Preston would decide to reward creativity when he'd always tried to discourage it in Patrice and others. Perhaps he had realized, at last, that striptease could incorporate innovation.

I went backstage to greet Vita.

"Hey, girl!" she called out. "You decided to come back."

My "two-week vacations" had become a running joke in the club. I took them whenever the pressures of the job got to me. Because I was a "marginal" dancer, neither highly motivated to rise in status nor highly esteemed by the management, I was allowed to come and go as I pleased. When I did put myself on the schedule, I came to work on time, hustled drinks, and complied with the club's rules. My presence helped to substantiate Preston's claim that stripping attracted middle-class college girls, and so he tolerated my periodic absences. I, in turn, used that middle-class privilege to reinforce my feeling of differentness from the other dancers. Their lives revolved around the job, I told myself; mine revolved around my relationships, school, and outside interests. I happened to strip for money; I was not a stripper.

"What's this about the most creative dancer?" I asked Vita.

"Oh, that," she scoffed. "That's one more gimmick to get you all at each other's throats. It's working, too. I came back here to the DJ booth the other day, and two girls were fussing and throwing records around. One of them was going, 'She played my song.' I told them, 'Hey, you all take this shit outside. You might hit me in the eye.' Isn't that the craziest thing, how they fight?"

"Yes," I agreed, glad that she exempted me from her judgment.

"Now don't get me wrong. I don't blame them. You learn how to fight down here. You can't let some guy go digging up your behind, up your dress, trying to kiss you, because Lord, you sure don't want nothing the doctor can't get rid of. You know, white men come in to see if black women look the same as white women do. Or they're curious to see if the woman will do any tricks for them; if they blow in your ear will you blow back? They all come in for something free. What I can't dig is this thing of dancers knocking each other, the same way men do. 'She don't got no titties. She don't got no ass.' That's stupid."

Vita stopped talking as the manager stormed into the DJ booth. "The music is too loud," he shouted.

"Is that better?" asked Vita, adjusting the volume.

"Now it's too low," he charged.

She switched back to the original volume.

"That's better," he said, and left.

"What's his problem?" I exploded. "That's how loud the music always is."

"I can't be precise enough nowadays," Vita said. She held

130

her fingers to her lips to silence me, and spoke into the microphone. "Thank you, Angelique, and thank you, Cinderella. Next up on our front stage, the Nudie-Tease is proud to present the lovely Miss Rebel Rawlins. And on the back stage, in the Bare Beaver Bar, please welcome Butterfly. That's Rebel Rawlins and Butterfly."

Before she'd even hung the microphone back on its cradle, the manager returned. "You mumbled into the microphone," he hollered. "You didn't pronounce your words properly."

"I'm doing my job exactly as I've always done it," Vita said icily.

"That's not good enough."

When he'd gone, Vita stammered, "I don't ask anyone to love me or like me, just to respect me. I'll tell you, it's hard to respect a man like that."

She started to alphabetize the record albums dancers had strewn around the room. Puffing furiously on a cigarette, she looked different than I'd ever seen her. I couldn't pinpoint the difference at first. She looked thin and wiry, nervous as ever. Then I noticed her hair. She'd let it curl into its natural state. And her eyes had no makeup on them. She'd shed her "Oriental" disguise.

She watched me as I registered the meaning of what she'd done. She explained, "Come summertime, it didn't do any good to press my hair. With the humidity, it frizzed right back up. So I let it go natural. Oh ho! Then they realized I was black. It used to be all politeness between us. I'd say hello to them, they'd say hello to me. And now, well, you saw."

"Why don't they just fire you? Why go out of their way to harass you?"

"Didn't I go out of my way to fool them? And didn't you ever hear of a token? Yes, baby, they're letting me feel black. I have five years of education behind me, with a bachelor's degree. They knew I wanted the head DJ slot. Did they con-

131

sider me for it? No. They had me train a dancer who knew nothing about the equipment for the job. I was qualified enough to train a head DJ but not to be head DJ."

"Vita, I think you should quit and get a better job."

"Will you feed my son while I'm looking? Or would you like to get unemployment compensation out of them for me? I'm disappointed, sure. It's hard for me to understand such bitter prejudice against blacks, and it's been getting to me. But I need this job. Do me a favor and don't stir up any trouble on my behalf."

"I'm silent," I promised.

As I got up to leave, I was swept back by an overzealous dancer. She wore a fluorescent orange feather boa. A melon-colored leotard covered her from neck to ankles.

"Where's my music?" she gasped. "My new costume, together with this tape—I'm going to win the contest."

I laughed. "To tell you the truth, Karma, this costume looks like all your others: orange." She worshiped an Indian guru who championed tantric yoga and sexual expressiveness. He also insisted that his devotees dress in orange. Several of his followers worked at the Nudie-Tease, and they all stripped out of orange costumes.

"It's not the same," she protested. "The boa cost me seventy-five dollars."

"Seventy-five dollars to see yourself on videotape?"

"And maybe a raise," she added.

That day, I saw what dancers had done to compete in Preston's contest. The women who wore orange bought new costumes in deeper shades of orange. The women who wore sequins bought new sequiny creations for twice the price they normally paid. They interpreted creativity as creative purchasing, and they fought over whose purchase would win the coveted prize. The usual sly derisions sharpened into outright insults. "That looks like something you peeled off the bottom of a barrel," Rebel said of another dancer's three-hundred-dollar dress. Songs, which had been public property, now "belonged" to the first person who played them. Dancers stood around in clusters to critique the skill of the woman on stage.

I retreated from the competition, feeling that I stood no chance of winning, no matter what I did. The winner would be a young woman whom Preston happened to fancy because of her blond hair, her awe of his power and eloquence, and her willingness to fall into the star pattern of buying expensive costumes that would reflect nicely on the club. Still, secretly, I wished that I could be that kind of woman. I resented that Preston did not value me as I was. I rejected the notion that only certain narrowly defined physical types qualified as beautiful, and yet I craved the attention and approval that blond hair, long legs, and gentile features would bring me. I refused to buy costumes or to straighten my hair, as Preston suggested I do. I panned all his rules when I spoke to the other dancers. I declined to act naïve and adoring when I spoke to him, although that affect may have endeared me to him. But I never challenged him to his face. Courteous and demure, I left open the possibility that he might someday realize my intrinsic worth.

Several months earlier, in an unprecedented show of unity, a group of dancers had challenged one of the lower managers. Too many dancers had been scheduled to work one day, and Warren wanted to send some of us home. We held a caucus in the dressing room and decided to have an all-or-nothing stand; either we'd all stay or we'd all go home. Everyone had her reasons for wanting to work: Tamara had driven down from Vermont; Jasmine's rent money had been ripped off; Monique needed money for her kid. When Warren heard about our union, he threatened to ban us all from every club in Boston. Tamara suggested that we choose who would stay and who would go, instead of giving Warren complete power over us. Then one woman said, "It's their club. We have to do what they say." One by one, we gave in. Warren handed down the decision and we obeyed.

That moment of solidarity contrasted sharply with the competition engendered by Preston's contest. Whereas, however briefly, we had been willing to sacrifice our jobs for each other, we now clawed and shoved to reach the pinnacle of status within the club. I had noticed other changes in the past few months as well. Preston had instituted a series of fines for various offenses. We could be charged for being caught with drugs, for dancing without the proper silver or gold spike-heeled shoes, and for lingering backstage for the first few seconds of our sets, precious seconds during which customers might decide to leave. Notices appeared around the club, signed, "the management," to remind us that we were ladies. Ladies must not leave empty glasses around the dressing room. Ladies must mix in evening gowns, not hot pants. Ladies really ought to do floor shows, and do them for exactly three minutes, showing the men enough to keep them interested but not enough to leave them feeling satiated. Written on official Nudie-Tease stationery, in the most formal and respectful tones, these notes served to remind us that we were part of an organization. The success of the entire operation necessitated our cooperation, these messages implied; we'd all benefit from the good reputation and net profits of the enterprise. The individual members of the ubiquitous "management" did not step forth to enforce their new rules. The rules hovered above us like the edicts of an invisible potentate. Disobedience would bring punishment, or worse yet, dismissal, but the hand that punished and dismissed remained unseen. It dipped into our pay envelopes or left notes for us telling us not to return to work the next day, but it left no fingerprints. We felt frustrated by the new laws, which were enforced in as uneven and capricious a manner as they had been before they'd been printed on official stationery.

Treated as unequal individuals, we looked for other individuals to blame for our frustrations. A dancer named Brandy received a note with her pay saying, "We won't be needing you anymore." She went to Victor to ask why. Victor sent her to Preston, whose reaction was, "Ask Victor." Then she turned on the other dancers, accusing us of tattling to the management about her use of cocaine.

We rumored that Preston had hired spies, and that these agents sat among us in the dressing room listening to our banter and complaints, only to report back to Preston what we said. We watched for the women who seemed to escape reprimand no matter what they did; they must be the tattlers. If a woman seemed to have classified knowledge of Preston's intentions, we accused her of being a double agent. Caught up in our self-enclosed web of allegations, we forgot the source of our discontent.

Preston may or may not have hired spies. He may have had a genuine desire to upgrade the management of the club for the good of his employees. Perhaps the theory, which several other dancers and I began to develop, that the new rules and regulations and the general atmosphere of distrust in the club had been created by the management to head off any attempts at collective protest, had no basis in fact.

Later, Preston himself told me, "Unions, historically, occur when there is a great deal of human suffering, a great deal of exploitation, and political powerlessness. I don't think, number one, that the girls are exploited. Number two, I don't think they're suffering. Number three, I don't think they're powerless. The status of the dancers at the Nudie-Tease is such that they would not benefit from unionizing. They have certain tax advantages as independent contractors. They get paid in cash; they're responsible for themselves to report their income, and that situation would change dramatically if they were to unionize."

Nonetheless, we had many complaints about the job. Every day in the dressing room, I heard dancers rail against the

135

conditions of employment. Even women like Rebel, who defended the profession, found fault in the club's policies.

"Working all these doubles wears me out," she confided. "They don't tell me I have to do it, but when they ask it doesn't have a question mark behind it."

If Preston didn't believe that we were exploited, suffering, or powerless, he did perceive a certain level of discontent among his employees. Rather than let us smolder, and perhaps organize, he held "dancers' meetings." "It's a place for dancers to air their general grievances, very often against one another," he explained. "It's a forum for them to complain about the behavior of their cohorts without being dishy, so to speak. They don't have to name names. They can just say, 'Some girls, I'm surprised at how they were brought up. There's all these dirty clothes in the dressing room, they never wash their underpieces, they pee in buckets in the ladies' room.' Are they having problems with a particular manager or bartender? What can and can't they do on stage? Is anybody helping them with makeup or wardrobe or grooming? It's a valuable tool for them to realize that the place exists in part for them."

None of us knew what to expect from the first meeting. Approximately thirty dancers sat around the Bare Beaver Bar at ten o'clock on a Saturday morning, many of us bleary-eyed because we'd worked the late shift the night before. While we waited for Preston to arrive, we sipped the coffee and ate the doughnuts he'd provided.

Looking around the room, I felt a sense of danger and excitement. We had come together to demand our rights. This meeting could mark the start of a new movement. Strippers, like prostitutes, could form a union, through which we could fight the law, unfair club owners, and battering boyfriends. I'd heard of such a union in Los Angeles. We could form a coalition and hold nationwide conventions.

"Are you okay?" Pandora asked me.

I realized that I'd been banging my fist on the bar. "Fine," I said.

I had forgotten that I worked as a stripper, and that my very job indicated a power imbalance between men and women. To stay at the Nudie-Tease, I would have to accept that men viewed me as a sex object. I'd have to enact familiar versions of femininity, which feminists thought of as oppressive, to get a rise out of my audience. To fight against those norms would be to destroy my job. Did I want to be a stripper or a feminist?

"Good morning, girls," Preston greeted us. Clean-shaven and chipper, he walked around the bar to an empty seat. Victor and Warren sat on either side of him.

For a moment I thought that we could be the employees of any firm. If we worked for an insurance company, we'd be similarly stratified, with men in the top positions and women as secretaries and file clerks. We could be a medical team, with Preston, Victor, and Warren as the doctors, and the rest of us as nurses, dietitians, and chambermaids.

But the topics on our agenda identified us as workers in a strip joint.

"We need more heat in the dressing room," a woman called out.

"And toilet paper in the ladies' room," someone else said.

"Please get rid of that new bartender, Albert. He scares my customers away."

We all directed our comments at Preston, who graciously nodded and promised to do what he could. We flung grievance after grievance at him, but we did so timidly, as if begging him to grant our wishes. No one dared to discuss the topics we discussed regularly in the dressing room. We asked for mild reforms, and never pointed to Preston as the perpetrator of the conditions we found unsatisfactory. No one questioned the hegemony of the management, even as its members sat across from us, a solid wall of authority.

Preston had a topic of his own to bring up: grooming. "The Nudie-Tease is an internationally known establishment," he boasted. "We've got some of the best-looking girls in the business. Every girl has some special feature, some quality she can bring out to her advantage. Some of you know how to do that better than others. I've asked Rebel, who is so excellent at applying her makeup, to tell us how she does it."

Thirty women silently glared at Rebel, who shifted uncomfortably in her seat. She began hesitantly. "I don't do any one thing. I keep my eye to my appearance all day long. You've got to wash your face real good, because of the smoke in here. I put on a moisturizer, and then a foundation. It's worth it to buy the best for your skin." She droned on about how she highlighted her eyes with three shades of eye shadow, and how she outlined her lips before coloring them in with lipstick.

Preston thanked her when she'd finished.

"We appreciated it," said a dancer named Ophelia, sarcastically.

She set the tone for the rest of the meeting. We began to tear each other down.

"Some girls sit around all day while the rest of us work our asses off mixing," Tulip said.

"Yeah, those of us who know how to talk to a guy should get first shot," Ginger insisted. "How can I invite a gentleman to have a conversation with me when some chick just split two seconds after he bought her a drink?"

"Those of you who have trouble with mixing should get pointers from the experts," Preston beamed.

"I got a thing or two to say about the costumes some girls wear," Rebel snapped. "Some of us spend money to look good on stage. Now how are we going to lift up the reputation of this place if other girls wear rags for costumes? I don't care what they wear outside of here. I don't want them dragging all of us into the gutter with them."

Preston nodded approvingly. "There's no reason for anyone

138

to wear torn or shabby costumes. We have several dressmakers who will design costumes for you at a range of prices. You should all take pride in your appearances."

I felt tricked by the managers' smiling and solicitous expressions. They were not making any concessions, but rather deflecting our discontentment. I wanted to say that we would not be fooled. The wish to keep my job silenced me. I dug my fingernails into my palms.

"You're investing in your own career by buying costumes," Rebel said. "The more you put into it, the more you get out of it."

I didn't intend to talk, but the words came out anyway. I addressed Preston. "That's not what happens. You've set it up so we'll compete."

The benign smile remained on his face. "Speak up, Lolita. What was that?"

I've already gotten myself fired, I thought; I may as well repeat it. "You've set it up."

"What?"

"You've set it up."

No one said a word. Preston looked around the room. Victor smirked. The other women stared at me. Panic-stricken, I could not remember my argument. I, too, sat silent, unable to back up my accusation.

Rebel broke the silence. "If you don't like your position, do something about it. Buy a costume."

"That's not what I mean," I said lamely.

"A lot of girls resent you when you move up in this job." Another dancer picked up on Rebel's strain of argument, and again the session deteriorated into an exchange of insults.

I stopped listening. Was I turning a personal problem into a public issue, mistaking envy of the star dancers for a legitimate cause to challenge the management? Perhaps I had become like the proverbial old spinster, who couldn't catch a man, and so condemned sex. The path to stardom might not be as arbitrary as I thought. There might, although I had not yet seen it, be something extraordinary about the stars that warranted their success. How unattractive, I thought, to snivel because I didn't have the looks or ambition to make it in a system that gave every woman a fair shot. And I did, in some way, want to make it. I wanted to dance most of my shows on the front stage because front-stage shows connoted high status. I did want the customers to clap after my dances; I'd have felt mortified if they'd been indifferent to me. I did wear makeup and perfume and nail polish to please them. I couldn't honestly say that I didn't buy into the system that I accused Preston of imposing on the dancers. I chose, after all, to work as a stripper; nobody forced me.

So why did I feel angry? Why did I feel threatened by Preston's rules and policies? Compared to many bosses, he was a model of fairness. Neither I nor anyone I knew had been sexually harassed by him. He paid us every Tuesday. We could call in sick as often as necessary. He allowed us to take breaks during our workday. If we wanted to confide in him about our personal problems, he would listen. He encouraged women to pursue higher education, allowing us to arrange our schedules to accommodate classes. He tolerated drunkenness and drug abuse on the job, and even urged women to seek help for those problems. In the case of accidental pregnancy, he'd advise us about where to go for safe, legal abortions. I couldn't simply dismiss him as an exploiter.

My thoughts went back and forth between self-reproach and anger. Each time I thought of some policy or attitude that enraged me, I'd ask myself why I let it bother me. Did I have any real principles or did I protest because my little ego had been wounded? Did I demand to be valued because a nasty finger poked me from the inside and said, 'You're valueless'?

But no, I couldn't afford to think that way. While I could admit to the desire for admiration, even the limited kind of admiration available at the Nudie-Tease, I couldn't let myself believe that I had invented that desire. Everything in the strip joint supported the fight to become the star, to capture a huge portion of a finite amount of attention. So much in my own experience of being female, as a child, as a teenager, and now as a young adult, supported that desire. Why, because I sought admiration, should I also have to accept poor working conditions and unjust policies? Damn straight, I told myself; I want this job, and I'm also furious about it.

Preston left the meeting smiling broadly. "Very successful," he announced.

That day, several dancers congratulated me for speaking out. "Way to go, Lolita," Sugar said. "You really stood up to him."

"Why didn't you back me up, if you agreed?"

"I need my job."

Charlene had attended the meeting. Obviously hung over, she'd sat in a booth drinking coffee. Patrice had sat across from her, staring as if no one else existed. I doubted that either of them had heard a word.

Charlene proved me wrong. She pulled me aside that afternoon, saying, "I try hard. I'm wearing both of my Desirees now. I need more money. Charlie, he wants it."

"Ask for a raise," I said. "You deserve one."

The next day, she told me that Preston had promised her a five-dollar raise if she would add a floor show to her act. Although she'd always doubted her coordination too much to attempt a floor show, she had agreed to try.

Patrice and I watched as she stretched out on the stage. Lying on her back, with her thighs pressed together, she fumbled to unhook her G-string. Her eyes were shut and her jaws were clenched.

"A real blonde!" exclaimed the businessman sitting next to us, as she pulled her G-string up toward her navel.

Charlene flashed a wan smile at him, as she lay spread-eagled and motionless on the stage.

"That's what I like," the man murmured.

Patrice's face displayed no emotion during the floor show, but her hands revealed a growing tension. Starting out curled softly upward on the bar, her fingers gradually tightened into fists.

"I wouldn't kick that out of bed," said Charlene's male admirer.

Suddenly, Patrice turned on him. "Get out of here. Go on! She's not a slab of meat, a hot cunt." She tried to push him off his barstool.

"What's this?" The man tried to regain his balance.

"You heard me," said Patrice. "Scram or I'll have you kicked out." Her face was bright red and contorted with fury.

"I'm going to complain about you." The man wagged his finger at her as he got up to leave.

Patrice sat quietly, until Charlene came over to hustle a drink from the man who had watched her floor show so avidly.

"Where is he?" Charlene asked.

"I got rid of him," said Patrice.

Charlene looked confused. "Why'd you do that? I need a drink."

"Not from him, you don't. He was treating you like his pet cunt."

"What are you talking about?" Charlene cried. "Why don't you leave me alone?"

Patrice looked up sharply. "I care about you. I don't want to see you treated that way."

"I don't like you." Charlene walked off, wringing her hands.

Patrice struggled to keep her composure. She wiped her eyes and took long breaths. Her chin quivered. I tried to think of ways to console her. But when she spoke, her words were political. "We should be able to get raises without degrading ourselves. I'll show Preston a five-dollar floor show."

Later that day, while Preston and all the other men watched attentively, she pulled out the rug kept at the side of the stage for floor shows. With an exaggeratedly seductive expression on

142

her face, she proceeded to do a series of push-ups, sit-ups, and isometrics. Then, putting her head on the floor and inching her toes up gradually, she pulled herself up into a full headstand. And there she stayed until the end of the song, wiggling her toes and parting her legs. Had there been mirrors on the ceiling, the men might have enjoyed her act. As it was, some of them sat sullenly, while others yelled out, "Show us some pink." Afterward, Preston had to concede that she had done a floor show, and he gave her a raise.

I felt uneasy about what Patrice had done. She had chosen a highly individualistic solution, getting around the club's rules without challenging them directly. The result might be a tightening rather than an elimination of the standards about floor shows.

But then everything in the Zone seemed indirect. The lure of female nakedness tricked men into spending large sums of money. The customers fantasized about women they did not know. Dancers approached customers with feigned interest. We drank water while pretending to drink vodka. We obeyed rules that were never voiced to us, but merely printed on paper and displayed in the dressing room. We all dealt with each other as if through a mist, as if in agreement not to question the reality of the promise of fulfillment held forth by the strip joint.

At times, I thought that only violence cut through the mist. When Victor cracked a skull against a hard surface, I didn't doubt the blood he'd drawn and the pain he'd caused. Behind all the other games, the flirting and withholding, bidding for and buying of favors, physical force prevailed. It kept in check the men whose passions had to be siphoned into narrow channels if the club was to benefit from their arousal. It protected the bodies of the women who were needed to entice the men into the club. Sometimes I welcomed the relief I found in being witness to extreme violence. At least I knew, then, that I worked in a strip joint in the Combat Zone, and not in a soft glamour spot on the Riviera, if such a place existed.

When I'd started working at the Nudie-Tease, I'd thought that all of the potential for violence in the club rested in the hands of Victor. He initiated and squelched the unrest. Later, Victor went through a stunning transformation, and I saw that my impression had been too simplistic. He fell in love with one of the dancers, and he stopped stalking the aisles looking for a fight. Instead, he'd sit at the managers' table with Lily. Watching them, I couldn't fathom how the hands that had banged an old man like John into unconsciousness could caress a woman so gently. I could almost believe that Victor had a soft heart beneath his toughness, as so many dancers maintained. Perhaps the motive behind his violence really had been to protect us, at any cost, from men he considered dangerous. Perhaps, when he found one woman to shelter, love, and cherish, he did not need to prove his manhood by protecting all of womankind. He let other men take over that function. Now, when fights erupted between patrons, or when customers harassed a dancer, several bartenders would leap over the bar to calm the disorder. At times they threw punches and drew blood. However, the intensity of these fights never equaled that of Victor's brawls. And so even violence, which had been a very real threat to the men in the club, became a largely symbolic gesture. It existed as a potential, and instead of being localized in the fists of one man, it was dispersed into the fists of many.

In comparison to these men's direct expression of anger, Patrice's ploy to get a raise seemed quite feeble to me. It was spoken in a language that had no clout in the Zone. It struck me as especially inadequate because I knew the stifled force behind it.

"Sometimes I cheer myself up by fantasizing taking a gun and shooting at all the bottles on the bar," Patrice told me. "I don't picture aiming at the men's faces, because they don't have faces. I picture shooting the bottles in front of them and having the glass explode in their faces."

144

Although her fantasy repulsed me in its explicitness, I understood its source. Without any legitimate means through which to make demands, she devised a relatively harmless way to avert her anger. Contrary to Preston's analysis, many of us did feel powerless and exploited, and we did seek to alleviate those feelings, even if we could not alter the conditions that caused them.

I became militant in my dreams:

> A woman is on the stage stripping. She is nine months pregnant, her belly huge, her breasts swollen with milk. The men are yelling, "Take it off," "Spread it, baby." All of a sudden, she squats on the stage. The noise is blocked out. She is in a timeless silence, and she begins to give birth. I am the midwife. After a long while, but an easy birth, the baby emerges. Suddenly, the time and the place come back into focus. The men are standing up, moblike, shouting at her and throwing bottles. The glass shatters all around her. I pick up a large shard of glass and cut the umbilical cord. The woman laughs and says, "First it was a weapon, now it's a tool. A little piece of glass."

In my waking state, I felt less certain of my mission. When I felt ready to challenge the conditions I found oppressive, I cut myself down with self-doubt. I resented the very premise of the job, the viewing of women by men, and yet I wanted the praise that being viewed sometimes brought me. I felt trapped at times, and angry, but I didn't know who or what trapped me, or at whom to direct my anger.

What did the other women at the Nudie-Tease do about their frustration? I wondered. As I'd seen in the meeting, they could turn it against each other. Or they could rage against their customers. Other women, like Vita, who had no customers to lash out at, turned their anger inward. Vita chainsmoked, bit her nails until they bled, and ate so poorly that she became anemic. Still other women tried to numb themselves with drugs and alcohol.

I finally took the latter approach. I had chosen to work at the Nudie-Tease, I told myself. I only hurt myself when I chased off customers, got on bad terms with my employers, and alienated the other women. To be a stripper, to be Lolita, I had to keep Lauri's ideas out of the club. I could not be a stripper and a feminist at the same time. To maintain the separation between my two selves, I had to anesthetize Lauri when I worked. Under the influence of enough cocaine, she could be silenced, and then Lolita could try to recapture some of the enchantment she'd felt when she'd taken the job three years earlier.

And so, when the winner of Preston's contest was announced, and I saw that he'd chosen a woman who put no effort into her dancing, but who had the right physical attributes and bought the right costumes, I traded my disgust and envy for a fifty-dollar half gram of cocaine. As I stood in the bathroom shoveling the powder into my nose, I told myself that the best woman had won, and that I must try harder to succeed in my chosen profession.

EIGHT

TO BE SWEET-SMELLING
ALL OVER HER BODY

Early one morning, I came to work for the express purpose of
looking at my body. Before any other dancers arrived, I wanted
the luxury of examining myself from all angles in the mirrors
that lined the walls of the dressing room. Although I did look
at my face every day while applying my makeup, I rarely had
a chance to see the rest of my body. I usually stood in front
of the mirror in full costume, to straighten the seams of my
stockings, or to tuck stray pubic hairs under the tiny triangle
of my G-string. My body, which I bared every day, felt unknown to me, and I feared that it had deteriorated, that it had
faults of which I was not aware. I wanted to know precisely
what the men saw when they looked at me.

I shut the door hurriedly and stripped out of my clothing.
How shall I proceed, I wondered, from head to toe or front to
back? No, I'd follow the sequence of the striptease, moving
from less to more intimate parts of my anatomy. In that way,
I'd come closest to seeing what the men saw.

I started with my face. It had grown thin since I'd started
snorting large quantities of cocaine. Tapering down from a

wide forehead to a narrow chin, it looked like a rather angular heart. In the new narrowness of my jaw, my lips looked huge. "I love full, sensuous lips," a customer had told me. Were mine sensuous or were they merely oversized? I'd have to ask Rebel how to apply lipstick to give them the illusion of thinness. Moving on, I noticed that my eyes, though myopic and inefficient, had their virtues. Large and blue, they received many compliments. If only I could get rid of the dark circles under them, which no amount of makeup concealed completely. But that imperfection paled in comparison to the marring effect of my nose. Not only did my nose have large pores, which remained no matter how religiously I applied astringents, but it curved ever so slightly over a bump. That bump, which I examined in profile, came straight from my father. Damn him. I wanted a tiny, turned-up nose, a button, a pug. This one made me unique, I consoled myself. Like my hair, it marked me as different.

In my legs I recognized less character. Muscular though thin, they lost their shape below the knee. I had tried dozens of exercises to develop my calves, to no avail. They simply had no curve. High heels deflected attention from them by accentuating the delicate but well-defined stretch of my Achilles tendon up the back of my lower leg. "You have very pretty ankles," my father had reassured me when I was fourteen. Many other men had repeated his words, and I believed them. My thighs, however, confused the matter even more. From the front they looked fine. Thin and well toned, they touched and curved inward. From the back, I saw as I twisted to see myself in three different mirrors, they threatened to give in to the plague of cellulite. In patches as wide as two inches in diameter, my skin dimpled and indented. My God, I was only twenty-one years old. How hideous to have little pockets of fat even on bone-thin limbs. I had seen it on other women but never suspected it of myself. How could any man be attracted to me when I had such a glaring defect?

Perhaps my breasts made up for it. Since they'd emerged when I was thirteen, I'd been proud of them. For a woman as small as me, they were quite large. "They're a handful," a customer had said. Although they were filled with chronic benign cysts, men couldn't see that. They looked healthy and firm, situated high up on my chest. Yet before I could accept them, I had to submit them to the test I'd heard several dancers discussing. A pencil placed under perfect breasts would fall to the floor; if the breasts sagged, the pencil would be caught under them. I tried it. My breasts let the pencil slip free. They were okay. I noticed that they looked best when I arched my back, thrusting my chest forward and my hips out to the rear. I must try to remember that posture.

In that posture, my buttocks looked best as well. "Did you know," Lamont had asked me, "that they are round and full although you are so thin?" If they didn't curve in the shape of an upside-down heart like the celebrated buttocks of the women in *Playboy*, neither were they flat. I had worried about that ever since a man on the street had insulted me. I'd been walking along in a good mood, humming a song. "You're flat," he'd said. "You mean I can't keep a tune?" I'd asked. "No, I mean your ass don't got no shape." But he was wrong. It protruded far enough to qualify as sexy. What if I stood with my back straight instead of arched? Aha, that's when it flattened out against my legs. I tried the pencil test with that part of my anatomy, as well, and passed by a thin margin.

Bending over, I looked between my legs at the reflection of my crotch in the mirror. "That's what we like," I could hear the men saying. "Do it over here." I wiggled my behind a little bit and then settled down onto the floor as if I were about to perform a floor show. Pretending that my reflection was me and that I was an attentive audience, I spread my legs. I should shave some of my pubic hair to give a better view, I judged. Or maybe not. It looked normal enough. But who really wanted to see a woman's genitals exposed so explicitly? "I like

149

to see as much as I can," I remembered a man saying. "Not to the point of gynecology, but anything up to that." "I'd never put my lips to one of them stinking things," another man had said. I flashed on the suggestive flower patterns of Judy Chicago's *Dinner Party*. Did my labia look like flower petals? Should they be brighter pink or smaller or more visibly excited?

As I lay there with my legs spread, making coy expressions at myself, I noticed the beginning of a pimple on the tip of my nose. Makeup would cover it only partially. It would be the first thing anyone noticed. To scrape or poke or pinch it would only worsen it. More pus would gather in my body to fill it, and it would erupt into a full-blown infection. It had emerged from inside me as an advertisement of my essential impurity, and I couldn't take my eyes from it.

"Well, I never!" Rebel shrieked as she entered the dressing room. "Lolita, what in the world are you doing?"

I jerked back from the mirror. "I'm looking at this zit I've got," I explained sheepishly.

"With your legs spread a mile wide? I swear, some girls are just plain weird."

"I was exercising." I felt chagrined to have been caught in that position.

"I don't know about ya'll," Rebel sighed. She dropped her makeup bag on the table and started to take off her clothes. Rubbing her hands along her depilated legs, she said, "They need a shave."

"I wish that was all my legs needed," I groaned. "They need a miracle."

Rebel rolled her eyes up to the ceiling. "Here we go again. 'I can't stand this part of me. God didn't do it right on that part.' The good Lord gave it to you, and that's all you need to know."

"You like everything He gave you?" I asked.

"Better believe it. I'm cute and I know it."

She ran her electric razor along the long muscles of her

calves, returning to certain spots to make sure that she'd gotten the stubble. Then, standing up, she looked at her legs in the mirror. "My tan's wearing off."

"How'd you get a tan in the middle of the winter, anyway?"

"Sun lamp. I sit under it every week, only this week I didn't have time."

"That's bad for you, don't you know?"

"Looks good, though. I wouldn't be caught dead up there naked without my tan."

She procured an eyebrow tweezer from her cosmetic bag and began to pluck at the barely perceptible nubs of hair between her brows. Ouch, she winced with each removal. When she'd finished, her eyebrows looked like two thin lines of color. Over them she penciled in thicker lines, copying a style from a glamour magazine sitting on the table.

With that done, she focused on her underarms. First she sprayed them with antiperspirant, next she powdered them, and finally she sprayed a long stream of perfume into them.

"Calm down," I choked. "We've got to breathe in here."

"That's exactly what I say," Rebel retorted. "Why don't you use some, too?"

"Did you know that antiperspirants make you go senile?"

"Little Miss Natural. Want to do some all-natural cocaine?"

"That sounds good," I agreed. "One hundred percent pure, right?"

We each did two lines. The sharp taste of the coke mingled with the smell of the deodorant to produce an acrid, chemical taste in my mouth. I puckered my lips, wondering how something that made me feel so good could wreak such havoc on my body. I'd lost ten pounds, never felt hungry, got nosebleeds fairly frequently, and had cold sores all over my mouth.

"I'll admit," said Rebel, "I do go in for some natural products myself. I discovered a strawberry douche I like pretty much."

"A strawberry douche?" I laughed.

"That's right, a woman should smell sweet, like flowers or fruit."

"You don't need a douche. Do men perfume their penises?"

"That's on the outside. It's the internal smells that need fixing. Same as using a mouthwash," she said with certainty.

"You don't like what's inside you?"

"Don't go making a big thing out of it. All I'm saying is that a true lady takes care to be sweet-smelling all over her body."

"For someone who thinks God made her perfect, you do an awful lot of shaving and plucking and covering up."

"God gave me a good body. That's not saying I don't need to keep it up. It's like if you have a car, it gets greasy and rusted on the inside and dirty on the outside, unless you tune it up and take it to the car wash. I look on my body like that."

"Well, who am I to talk," I conceded. "I just feel hopeless about some parts of mine."

We both glanced up as Charlene walked into the dressing room. As Rebel and I had done, she dropped her purse on the table and took off her clothing. No visible bruises today, I observed. She still wore her hair in the banana curls Rebel had fashioned. They dangled around her face. Her makeup looked garish; it stood out stark against the white skin of her neck, which looked even paler than usual.

"As I was saying," Rebel continued. "You know my motto: nothing's hopeless, not even you."

"Hopeless?" Charlene repeated vaguely.

"No, nothing's hopeless, honey," Rebel reassured her. "My, don't your curls look nice today? If you want someone to be jealous of, Lolita, here's your girl. She's a peach."

"I'm a blond bombshell," Charlene said, quoting some man, no doubt.

I glared at her enviously. Why couldn't I be a "blond bombshell"? I didn't want to be Charlene, with her drinking and violent boyfriend; I just wanted to inhabit her body, to be the bomb inside her shell. She had, in her physique, everything I'd always wished for, and she didn't appreciate it. I couldn't admire her, as I might admire an attractive man. I wanted to possess and destroy her, annihilate her identity and replace it with mine. I wanted her long blond hair to sweep over my shoulders. I wanted to run my tongue over lips that curled and pouted exactly like Marilyn Monroe's. Those legs, which touched at thigh, calf, and ankle, as the magazines said they should—I wanted them below my own hips. And what right had she to breasts so lovely, ample, and firm?

The customers loved her breasts. In adulatory tones, they spoke of an imaginary second infancy in which they could spend their days with their faces pressed against her bosom. There, they'd inhale her milky scent and know that they'd found a haven in a world which demanded that they always behave as men. At the same time, they would be men as they pursed their lips around her nipples and reached forward with their hands and tongues to excite her. "That's where I'd find peace," a man had told me, pointing to Charlene's breasts. Then, as if to explain, "Of course, I'm a breast man."

Some customers saw Charlene as a kind of virgin mother. To her, that role was as good as any other. It even excused the effects of the alcoholic fog in which she walked around. She could forget to take anything off during the first half of her show, and a murmur would rise in the audience about her goodness and modesty. Or she could take everything off in the first five minutes of her act, and the men would speak of the innocent abandon with which she stripped. She'd worn her southern belle costume since the day Rebel had handed her a new image. Cloaked by the yards and yards of white fabric, she looked ravishing. The bodice pressed her breasts together to form a soft line of cleavage. She looked both fecund and chaste, waiting to be touched and capable of delivering a gift, a child, a fantasy that would offer the men in the audience some hope for their own futures.

Although I knew that she had been "touched" by Charlie,

I thought of her as an abused child rather than as a battered woman. By seeing her as controlled by people and forces outside of herself, I felt self-reliant in comparison. If I felt some compunction about knowing of her problems and doing nothing to help her, I assured myself that domestic problems were private. I wanted to believe the face she presented and the character she played on stage. And so, when her breasts began to swell, when blue veins appeared through their translucent veil of pale skin, and when her nipples darkened from light pink to reddish brown, I didn't think that she might be pregnant. I thought, only, that her breasts looked riper, ready to be touched, and I felt even more envious.

"If these tits keep on growing hairs, they're going to need electrolysis," Rebel said as she brought the tweezers down to her breast.

"What tits?" I asked, noticing that she spoke of the parts of her body as if they were not parts of her: the legs, the tits.

"The ones sitting on my chest," she pointed. "These ones here."

Charlene stood by her locker preparing to go on stage. She struggled to fit into her dress, unable to pull the zipper up over her hips. "Can you help me?" she asked Rebel. "I ate a big breakfast."

"That and a big dinner last night," Rebel said as she tugged at the zipper. "Hold in your stomach."

"It won't go in any more," Charlene whimpered. She reached up into her locker to find her bottle of Southern Comfort.

"Put that away," Rebel shouted. "You'll make it worse."

Just then I heard the unmistakable sound of ripping cloth. Turning, I saw that the dress had split in the middle of the fabric. The hole exposed several inches of Charlene's skin.

"Look what I did," Rebel cried. "Your beautiful dress. I'll get it fixed for you. Tomorrow I'm taking it to Eddie the Tailor."

"It doesn't matter," said Charlene. "I didn't like this dress once I started wearing it, anyhow."

She put on an older, looser dress and left the dressing room to go on stage.

"Did you see that?" Rebel whispered to me as soon as Charlene had left.

"That she's getting fat?"

"She wasn't wearing any underpieces under the white dress, and just now she went on stage without any. If that isn't the most vile, rude thing I ever saw."

"Big deal."

"It is a big deal if you've got any pride." Rebel gathered together her paraphernalia and stalked out into the bar.

When I left the dressing room several minutes later, the uncustomary silence in the bar caught my attention. Charlene walked aimlessly around the stage, as she always did, but the men sat quietly. A few of them walked out of the club, leaving unfinished drinks. Others turned their eyes from the stage. One man spoke, at last, barking out the word "cunt." Charlene grimaced but continued to walk down the runway.

"Someone ought to tell her," Rebel said, coming to stand beside me.

"Tell her what?"

"It's downright disgusting, and she's bringing us right down with her."

Then I saw the cause of all the commotion. A thin line of blood trickled down the side of Charlene's left thigh. Crimson and brilliant against her white skin, it zigzagged almost down to her knee. She gave no sign of noticing it, although her face looked pained and colorless.

Vita stood in the wings gesturing wildly to Charlene to come backstage. By chance, Charlene saw her and obeyed. I went, as well, to see what was going on.

Vita sent a dancer on stage to replace Charlene, sent another

woman to "make a phone call," and began to question Charlene.

"You got your period?" she asked.

Bewildered, Charlene reached down and felt the blood
against her thigh. "I must. I don't know."

"You've got to know," Vita insisted. "When was your last
one?"

"I don't know. Long time ago, a few months."

"Are you pregnant?" Vita pressed.

Charlene buckled over in pain. "I think so."

"You think so! You gonna let it grow in you for nine months,
and then one day it pops out and you're a mother? That ain't
how it works, sugar. What kind of mother are you going to
make, drinking like you do? You better wake up."

"I want a little baby," Charlene said. "Charlie'll marry me."

"He hasn't married you yet," said Vita softly. "Now listen
to me. I'm a mother and I know. You all forget down here that
you are women, and these things happen. You don't have that
body just so you can look good and make men feel all cozy when
they get inside you. You've got a growing fetus inside you now.
What are you going to do about it?"

"They like my boobs better big like this," Charlene said.

"Go on the pill if you want big boobs. Don't bring a child
into this world."

Charlene grimaced again as the blood began to flow more
heavily. She cried softly and held her knees up to her chest.

"The Lord made the decision for you this time," Vita
soothed her. "Come on, now. Lie out here on the rug. We're
getting you some help. There's help on the way. You're going
to be fine."

I ran to the bathroom, afraid that the sight of blood might
make me vomit. It wouldn't in any other setting, but menstrual
blood didn't belong in the Zone. We did our best to hide it.
I'd seen it on stage only once before, and that woman had been
so ashamed of her leaky tampon that she'd quit the job. An-

156

other woman had ceased menstruating altogether, and her doctors couldn't explain why. Even Patrice and I, who professed to accept the natural processes of our bodies, carefully cut the strings from our tampons and washed ourselves to remove traces of blood.

Motherhood didn't belong in a strip joint. I remembered a story Nina had told me about a club in Wisconsin. A dancer had recently given birth, and her breasts had been filled with milk. On stage, she had twirled and manipulated her breasts so that milk had come forth and rained out into the audience. The men had been horror-stricken. They'd covered their heads with their arms. "This can't be happening to me," one man had sworn. When I'd heard that story, at the age of sixteen, I'd found it amusing. Now I understood it. The ability to conceive and give birth, like every other aspect of female sexuality, had a different meaning in a strip joint. It existed as a male fantasy. The customers had dreamed of Charlene as a mother, and she had accepted their static, clean, and unbloodied image of motherhood. When she'd gotten an actual fetus inside her, she'd been unable to cope with it. She'd continued to drink alcohol and to eat inadequately, until her body had ejected the fetus.

Patrice had been in New York working on a show for several weeks. When she returned, I told her about Charlene's miscarriage. I expected her to launch into a sermon about the damage done to women by men. Instead, she sat down heavily at the bar and began to twirl her black hair around her fingers. She laughed a thin, disconnected giggle. "I don't know, I don't know," she said. "Now I've got banana curls. Now I'm Charlene."

"What the hell are you talking about?"

"Charlene and I have more in common than I ever knew."

"You do?"

"Here's a fairy tale," she said, leaning over so close to me that I could feel her breath. "Once upon a time, three weeks

157

ago, Patrice went to New York to make it big in the theater. She was paying her bills by dancing in a little bar up in Spanish Harlem. Big and brave. Except she was afraid to hail a cab or walk the three blocks to the subway at two o'clock in the morning. One night, the manager told her, 'My friend here can give you a ride home.' Patrice knew better. But she also knew she'd insult the manager if she said no, and he hadn't paid her yet. So she took the ride. Her 'escort' drove her through streets she'd never seen before. He grabbed her thigh and unzipped his fly. Started jerking off. Grunt, grunt. Patrice felt terrified. But not really. She was thinking, 'Oh, this is what terror feels like. I'm an actress. I can use this.' She tried to get back into the skin of Anita, the tough, city-bred Hispanic woman she'd played that day. 'You're gonna take me home,' she told the man. Her voice! Patrice had always imagined that if a man attacked her she'd let loose with this Amazon wail; she'd bellow, she'd scream. No go. Her voice came out as a whisper. What would Anita do? She'd leave. So in the middle of Harlem, Patrice leaped out of the car. The man kept circling the block. Finally she got back in the car; Anita wouldn't stand out on that street corner in the middle of the night. Anita would appeal to his macho. 'You gave your word to your friend.' He just grabbed her thigh again. Okay, then appeal to his racism. 'Get me out of this black neighborhood.' He understood that. Started driving downtown. He stopped at a red light by Forty-second Street. Aha. Patrice spotted a police car idling by an empty building. She jumped out of the car. Now, she must not use her overeducated white bitch privilege to get help. She must stay in character. She'd play Anita, the way she'd learned in acting school. She knew what she wanted and why she couldn't have it, and she used the conflict to drum up dramatic action. Anita didn't know the English word for rape. She ran up to the cops and said, in her Spanish accent, 'This man is trying to do bad things to me. I want you to arrest him.' Anita, alone at three in the morning, with her garish makeup on. The cops told her, 'Now, honey, don't get upset.' They ate their Dunkin' Donuts and listened to their radio. Escort drove off. So Patrice caught a cab and went home. The end."

"That's awful," I said. "But why'd you tell it to me now?"

She threw her hands up in the air. "Who am I? Who's Charlene? How are we ever going to talk to each other?"

"I don't know," I said, confused.

Patrice stood up and clapped her hands together excitedly. "That's where to start. I'll tell her all this." Smiling, she went to get dressed for the stage.

A few days later, she squatted by her locker in the dressing room. Wearing street clothes and no makeup, she was stuffing her costumes into a plastic trash bag.

"Laundry time?" I asked.

"Quitting time."

"So you talked to Charlene?"

"She did most of the talking. She doesn't think she's like me, because I'm a queer; she's a woman. I'm an insect that wants to crawl all over her body. She spit on me so I wouldn't come near her. Wouldn't even let me in the house. She sounded like she took lessons from Rebel. Stood at the door screeching, 'You want my body. You want to ruin me.' She's right."

"Don't give me that. You love her."

Patrice's eyes were red from crying, but there was a calmness about her. Her hands were still, her voice lower than before. She said, "I can't love her in the Zone. Here I feel sorry for her. I want her to suffer, so she'll need me. And if she needs me, maybe I'll be somebody. Is that love?"

I looked away.

She went on, "The longer I stay at this job, the more I want Charlene. But, you know, I used to want to hold her, and now I want to look at her. My own little Marilyn Monroe. Well, that puts me on the wrong side of the battle. I want to love women, not hurt them."

"Is this theory or you?"

"It's me, whoever that is." She stuffed the last of her costumes into the bag and stood up to go. "Right now I just feel like a dirty animal. That's how I felt with the man in New York, and when Charlene spit on me. This job made me into a cesspool. So I quit." She extended her hand to me, and took mine with a firm grip. "You should too."

When she'd gone, I leaned against the wall thinking about what she'd said. "A dirty animal." I understood that feeling. Every day I left the club feeling soiled.

Despite Preston's efforts to keep his club "clean," dirt clung to its open surfaces. Swept in from the street, the filth on which no one thought to clean, it colored everything gray. The men never had to touch it; they were fully dressed. The dancers, however, rubbed bare skin against dirty surfaces all day long. We leaned our elbows on sticky bar counters and pressed our naked bodies against stage mirrors covered with dust, sweat, and greasy fingerprints. During floor shows, we rolled around on the same planks we had just stepped on. We got fungus infections on our skin, and outbreaks of scabies spread like wildfire.

Then there were the traces of human contact, not always dirty in an objective sense, but undesirable because they'd been unasked for. Men stroked our arms with the same hands they'd just masturbated with in the men's room. They leaned over to kiss us with lips wet with beer and breath foul from liquor and cigarettes. They clasped our palms with hands sweaty from the excitement of finally touching a woman.

My overwhelming desire, when I left the club each night, was to purge myself of the unpleasant vestiges of my day's work. I'd shower and scrub to remove the sweat and soil. Always thinking of new parts of my body into which dirt might have crept, I took care to reach them all. I washed my face with a cleanser that promised to expel the oil from the deepest recesses of my pores before it even accumulated. I scraped the flaking skin from my legs and back with a rough sea sponge.

160

My hair, which tended toward brittleness anyway, suffered from exhaustion under my daily regimen of washing. Even after I'd gone to bed at night, I'd remember some spot I'd neglected to clean, and I'd jump up to wash it before falling asleep.

I also wanted to clear my mind of the many phrases and impressions that remained with me after work. Some of them I'd write in Lolita's journal. I filled the pages of those books with conversations I'd had with customers, descriptions of other dancers, and ideas I'd had about the meaning of the strip joint. I packed these accounts with the sense of melodrama and significance that the heavy use of cocaine helped me to find in every minute detail. What I didn't write down I told myself to forget. I wanted to free myself from the flashing reminders of the job that infiltrated my dreams and waking thoughts.

No matter how many purges with water and pen I put myself through, the job left its mark. The emphasis I placed on physical attractiveness had intensified since I'd worked at the Nudie-Tease. And the thought I finally consoled myself with, the thought that I could contain within myself the unsavory traces I couldn't eradicate, I had learned in the Zone as well. There, the only thing that counted was what one could see, and the belief that who one was and who one pretended to be could be separated, prevailed. To the extent that I believed that I could leave the events I experienced in the Nudie-Tease behind the club's doors, I accepted the identity of "stripper."

NINE

THE ROOT OF
THE PROBLEM

Lamont and I lay on my bed at midnight. We were about to undress when the telephone rang.

"Ignore it," I whispered.

"No one's here?" Lamont asked. "That's a first. Five roommates and an empty house."

"They went to New York for the weekend."

The telephone continued to ring.

"Maybe you should get it, love," he said. "I won't budge."

"Not an inch." I ran out to the hall on the seventh ring. "Hello?"

"Lolita?" I shuddered; someone from the Zone knew my number. "This is Charlene."

I'd forgotten that after her miscarriage I'd given her my number, saying I'd help her find a good doctor. "It's awfully late, Charlene. Can you call me tomorrow?"

"Tomorrow?" she drawled. "Won't you talk to me for a minute now?"

"What about?"

162

"I don't know," she faltered. "I wanted to tell you something. You're my friend, aren't you, Lolita?"

"Sure," I said noncommittally.

"I don't think I'm going to get my dress fixed. It tore so bad."

"That's what you called me about in the middle of the night?" I exploded. "Your costume?"

I heard her crying quietly on the other end of the line. In the background I heard a siren and a din of voices.

"Will you help me?" she asked.

"Where are you?"

"In a phone booth. In the Zone."

"Are you working tonight? Why don't you use the phone in the club?"

"Preston sent me home. I drank too much. He got mad."

"You've got to stop drinking so much," I said, feeling some concern; if Preston had to send her home, she must be in bad shape.

"What will I do?" she cried. "It's the only good thing I have. All you girls, my friends. I'm trying to do better. I'm buying a new dress instead of fixing up the old one."

"Maybe you should quit, before he fires you," I said. "You've been wanting to get out of it since the day I met you. I remember five years ago in the Twilight Lounge, you said it was a matter of weeks before Charlie got you out."

"I need the job." Her voice sounded shaky. "I'll be in trouble if I lose it."

"Let Charlie work for a change."

"Charlie," she scoffed. "There is no Charlie."

"You had another fight?"

"No." A recorded voice warned us that we'd be disconnected if Charlene didn't insert another nickel. "Oh God!" she gasped. "I must have one. Here, I can't see. I think it's a dime."

"Did he leave you for good this time?"

163

"There never was a Charlie. I made him up."

"You're drunk. Of course there's a Charlie."

She insisted, "I made him up. I felt better, pretending."

"All right, so let's pretend you made him up," I went along with her. "Now what? Why'd you call me?"

"I'm scared, if I lose this job. Can I come stay with you? I won't get in the way much. For a little while?"

"Are you crazy? I have five roommates. It's crowded here." We could have put her up in the living room; we often had visitors. But the thought of having her in my house upset me. It would be an invasion of the job into the rest of my life. I didn't even want to be on the phone with her.

"He might kill me," her voice trailed off.

"You just said there is no Charlie."

"Not Charlie."

"Who then? Are you seeing some guy from the club? You get those bruises from somewhere. Who's beating you up?"

She retreated. "I fall down a lot."

If I knew the real reason, I might have to commit myself to helping her. I said, "You shouldn't drink so much that you can't even walk. Take care of yourself. I'm kind of tired. Let's say good night."

"Wait!" I waited, and she stammered, "Not yet. I want to ask you something."

"What?" I asked edgily.

A siren went off in the background. She spoke loudly over it. "Lolita, I remember one time you told me about a college where you get credit for your life experiences. Do you think I could?"

That she could still look ahead to school, as beaten as she was, amazed me. As I thought of her strength, I also thought of her beauty, and I wanted her far away from me. I didn't want her to have all the options I had; I was the college girl.

"I doubt they'd want to give you credit for stripping," I said.

"I didn't think so. I don't know. Maybe I'll go back to New Jersey. This isn't me, anyway, not what I'm really like."

"What are you really like?"

"You know what my real name is? Not Charlene. It's Sue. What's yours, Lolita?"

"That's my name."

"Come on. You're my friend, aren't you?"

"I'm tired, Charlene. We can talk tomorrow, okay? Are you going to be all right?"

"Fine," she mumbled into the receiver. "Good night."

I went back to bed feeling both disturbed by Charlene's problems and resentful that she had intruded into my outside life. Clearly, she needed help, but I couldn't help her. She ought to talk to a social worker.

Lamont lay in the flickering light of the candle he had lit. Still dressed, he leaned on his elbow against the pillow. He extended his hand to me as I walked into the room.

I let myself be pulled toward the bed. I love this man, I thought; he needs me and I need him. Without me, he'd be lonely. He had no family and he isolated himself in his house. Like most men, he was buddies with the guys in the park, and he got his emotional needs met with a woman. With me, he could sit for hours holding hands and exchanging vows of love. He could also yell and release thirty-five years of accumulated anger, knowing I'd stay to hear it. Later, he could ask for solace in my arms, and I would hold him. I, in turn, could feel wanted. He picked me up from work, protecting me from the dangers of the Zone. He shielded me from the loneliness I would feel if I stripped all day and had no man to return to. With him, I could still feel some of the passions I had tried to dull at work.

At times I felt too much. I expected my personal life to provide me with a sanctuary from the impersonal marketplace in which I worked. If other men saw me only for my body, I wanted Lamont to value my mind. If my bosses demanded

165

perfection of me, I wanted Lamont to accept me unquestioningly. He could never do enough to satisfy me. We spent three nights out of the week together, and I wanted five. If he said he loved me, I wanted him to say he loved me more than any woman he had ever known. I missed him intensely when we were apart. I felt lovable because he loved me and sexual because he made love to me. I couldn't imagine surviving without him.

We had clung to each other from the start. He'd been newly divorced, and I had craved a serious relationship. For the first year, we were inseparable. We slept together every night. I cooked dinner for him, and he made pancakes for me in the morning. We studied together in the library at school. We each felt misunderstood by the world around us and felt that in the other we had found someone who could appreciate us. We retreated from politics into a private affair. Our friendships with other people dropped off as we secured ourselves in romantic isolation.

In that isolation, things began to decay. He suspected me of infidelity, accusing me of flirting with ex-lovers and men from the Nudie-Tease. I resented his unwillingness to look for full-time work, his dependency on my income. He declared that he could no longer be monogamous with me, that he must "feel divorced." I pressured him to live with me. Our moods shifted and crossed. I'd sink from mania to dejection as the cocaine I'd snorted wore off. His moods seemed even more capricious, like unpredictable departures from an overall state of depression.

Throughout most of the turmoil, we remained attracted to each other's bodies. We could not be together without touching. Neither of us wanted to be alone; through sex we thought we could possess and hold one another. He loved my smallness, which he saw as vulnerability. He'd kiss me inch by inch and tell me how perfect, how pleasing he found me. I'd do the same with him. The sinews of his legs, the breadth of his back, the smoothness of his skin, delighted me. I had never trusted my

166

body as completely to any other man, nor had I felt the intensity of pleasure I could feel with Lamont. I treasured the body which gave me that gratification.

In the last year, even our attraction had begun to fade. We'd begun to find flaws in each other's bodies.

"Who was that?" he asked.

"A stripper."

"Jesus! Won't they ever leave us alone?"

"I unplugged the phone," I said. "Now we're alone."

I kissed his closed eyelids. He'd turned thirty-five that month, and it was beginning to show. The lines around his eyes were etched in deeply, as were the furrows in his forehead. I smoothed the creases with my lips, and then pressed my mouth to his. As we kissed, he slipped his hands under my shirt to caress my breasts. In one smooth movement, he lifted my shirt over my head. "So beautiful," he breathed into my ear.

My mind shifted to the Nudie-Tease. Just a day before, as I'd stood on stage and bared my breasts, a man had sighed, "They are beautiful." His wizened face had spread into a wide smile, and he'd held his hands out on the bar like two cups. To transform his admiration into self-love, I'd done to myself what he might have liked to do to me. I'd held my breasts in my hands and excited my nipples until they stood erect. Then I'd turned away from him. To be desired by every man in the room and give myself to none seemed like the greatest victory I could win there. If I gave in and communicated with the men, they might see that I was not really Lolita, and thus not sexy or deserving of their admiration. I must give nothing to them but the privilege of looking at me, as I took in their praise.

"What are you thinking about, love?" asked Lamont.

I had drifted off, forgetting that the man by my side would not be satisfied by the mere act of admiring me. I must interact with him and enjoy myself to keep him with me. Besides, as I reminded myself, I loved him and wanted to please him.

167

"I was thinking of the first time we made love I lied. I seduced you."

"I thought I seduced you."

"You wanted to drink herbal tea. I had to drag you into the bedroom."

He laughed. "That's not how I'd describe it. You were busy telling me about being a stripper. I had to lure you into bed."

"However it happened, it was good. Imagine the first time I kissed these lips"—and I kissed him, thinking of that night.

"Remember the first time I unhooked your skirt, like this?" He repeated the motions.

"And I unzipped your pants."

I tried to feel the sensations of our initial lovemaking. I did feel a kind of pleasure, an enjoyment centered outside of my body. As Lamont slipped his tongue around my navel, a mild tingling began to build in my body. Starting in my belly, it extended in all directions at once. Then it stopped, as if it reached a wall of resistance, and a numbness replaced it. How do we look? I wondered. If there'd been a mirror overhead, it would have revealed two bodies intertwined, bellies fluttering with the rapid intake of breath, eyes rolled back, lips parted in private smiles. It would reflect all the postures and responses of sexual pleasure. So I must be feeling turned on. Lamont trailed kisses down my torso and along the insides of my legs. As he approached my calves, my muscles tensed. I wished he'd pass over them quickly and move on to more shapely parts of my anatomy. I pointed my toes to heighten the curve of my arch. With the deliberateness of growing arousal, he traveled back up my legs. I tried to relax as he pulled my underwear down over my ankles. The thought formed in my head, and grew until I could think of nothing else: am I clean? I hadn't worked that day, and so hadn't showered.

"Don't do that," I begged.

He didn't stop. If I pretended to enjoy it, maybe he'd stop sooner.

"Is it good?" he paused for breath.

"So good."

I remembered the shout of a man at the Nudie-Tease during one of my floor shows. "That's eating material." How did he know? I might have the stench so many men attributed to women's genitals. Worse yet, there might be visual evidence of my uncleanliness. As I'd removed my G-string I'd worried. Had I checked carefully enough? I'd twirled around on my hips, with my legs spread, to look in the mirror. Trying to be casual about it, I'd peered at my reflection. "Turn around," a man had yelled. "You gonna show it to us or not?" He'd gotten up to leave.

Lamont lay very still at my side.

"So good," I moaned automatically.

He looked quizzically at me. "What's good? Where'd you go off to?"

"I'm into it, love. Really. Let me show you."

As I kissed him, I asked myself why I felt numb. I loved Lamont. When we were apart, I often fantasized about making love to him. In those fantasies, I imagined the two of us in a series of suggestive poses. I pictured each pose as a separate frame in a movie, and took pleasure in the thought that we looked good together. If I tried to inject any fluidity into the fantasies, any movement from one pose to another, I lost interest. Lovemaking, in my mind, became like a floor show for two people, an act, the "sex act." I could no longer locate myself in my body. I watched myself and imagined being watched. The excitement I must feel and impart to satisfy Lamont seemed extraneous to the aesthetic purpose of our act.

Still, I must pretend, even if his writhings and noises struck me as absurd. I stripped him down to his socks, wishing it were over. Too many thoughts distracted me. Images from the Nudie-Tease appeared with no conscious evocation. I tickled Lamont's back with my fingertips. He sighed contentedly. I reached down to remove the last of his clothing, his socks.

They smelled slightly sweaty. An irrational fury consumed me. I threw the socks against the wall and shouted, "Why don't you take a shower?"

Lamont bolted upright. "Who the hell do you think you are, telling me what I need to do?"

"I work around dirt. You think I want to come home to it?"

"Hey, nobody tells you to work in that strip hole." He was already standing up and putting his clothes back on.

"You don't respect me. Any other woman you'd be clean for."

"Listen, 'Lolita,' don't project your guilt onto me. I don't want to hear it. This shit you're spouting has nothing to do with me."

"Go to hell," I sobbed.

"I'm going, fast as I can get out of here. I'm not putting up with this. No more, baby. This is it." He pulled his socks back up and began to tie his shoelaces.

I watched him, not quite believing that he'd leave. When he put his coat and hat on, I began to panic. "Where are you going?" I asked innocently.

"Now she's sweetness personified."

"Please, Lamont, let's talk. Don't leave me alone here. Please talk to me."

"I can't talk to you, not now, anyway." And he left.

As I sat at the top of the stairs watching him go, I thought that just as he'd tried to get from me more passion and involvement than I could give, he now tried to take from me the security he thought I needed for survival. Well, he was wrong. I'd be all right. I'd do some coke. Like hell I needed him. Lolita might, but not me. And Lolita was a seductress; she could find another man. I felt a pain in my gut. Yes, it was Lolita begging and supplicating to hold on to a man who showed her no respect. I drew my strength from other sources. The pain grew stronger. I snorted a lump of cocaine; it shot into the back of my throat like a pellet. As the pain subsided, I told myself that

170

I could still make a separation between my work and my real life. I thought of Charlene, and I said aloud, "I've got to."

Walking into the kitchen, I felt grateful for my surroundings. Located in Cambridge, in a neighborhood that had long been populated by students and families who couldn't afford much rent, my home represented to me a challenge to the values put forth in the Zone. If glamour and plushness symbolized a stripper's success, then I had failed to become a stripper. My apartment, which I shared with five men and women, had the characteristic look of downward mobility. We'd furnished it with the heirlooms of one roommate's wealthy relatives, along with tattered relics taken from trash heaps. For decorations, we'd tacked up Indian print bedspreads over the peeling walls. We washed the floors when we got around to it, and used the dishwasher only when every dish had been soiled. Not wanting to give our money to profit-hungry corporations, we shopped at the food co-op. Some of my roommates played music for a living. Others got paid to think; they were intellectuals. They'd never been in a strip joint. I prized their ignorance of my workplace as a sign of my ability to keep separate the strands of my life.

Far from forgetting the Zone in my off-hours, I fashioned my life in reaction to it. When I got home from work, I often felt compelled to tell my roommates what I'd seen. "Patrice played a leprechaun today." "Rebel hauled off and punched a guy who grabbed her." My roommates responded uneasily to this introduction of the strip joint into their lives. They told me about job opportunities they'd heard of. A male roommate teased me, leaving telephone messages for Lolita. In spite of my avowed intention to keep separate home and workplace, the boundaries began to merge.

Likewise with my schooling. I'd completed my degree in counseling and made a half-hearted attempt to find a job in the field. Held back by the feeling that I could not pass in the "straight" world because my years of stripping marked me as

171

deviant, I'd decided to return to school. I took a course entitled "Women and Society." It was a revelation. Not only, I learned, did women earn only fifty-nine cents for every dollar earned by men, but a tradition and an ideology supported that inequality. That ideology, namely male supremacy, made the stripper a natural complement to the "good girl," rather than a deviant or an anomaly. Yes, my job had meaning! The more I learned about it, the angrier I became. When Preston continued to thwart the dancers' rumblings of protest with a skillful use of management techniques, I could pull from my readings in feminism an analysis of what he'd done.

My father applauded my newfound feminism. "To think," he said, "that only five years ago you thought so little of yourself that you worked in that low-class sleazy strip joint. And now you're writing papers about the radical reconstruction of gender roles. You've come a long way, kid."

I searched his voice for a sign that revealed his knowledge of my work. He must know. How did he think I supported myself? Several years back, I'd told him of my experiences at the Twilight Lounge. I'd promised him that I'd never strip again. Now I went to great lengths to hide the truth from him. Our silences became longer. I had nightmares that he'd walk into the club and discover that I stripped. My father, also afraid to know the truth, never asked.

I told my mother what I did, knowing that she had no authority over me. She saw stripping as the end result of my father's permissiveness. As I continued to strip long beyond what she termed an acceptable period of adolescent rebellion, she became seriously worried about me. Not only was I endangering myself physically, she'd say, but I was subjecting myself to the worst degradation possible. How could I, an avowed feminist, justify my actions? Why didn't I find a practical job and straighten up?

"You're a hypocrite," Nina charged.

"I'm adaptable."

172

"I call it hypocrisy when you spout off about sexism and then work to perpetuate it."

"Sexism is everywhere," I argued. "It's not confined to the Zone."

She looked exasperated. "Okay, the truth is I'm scared for you. I want you to quit before you get killed. Get it into your head: It's dangerous down there. Men come in expecting something, and when they don't get it they lash out, at the women, of course."

"Nina, bruised fruit doesn't sell. The bosses protect me and Lamont picks me up from work."

"Listen to you! 'Bruised fruit doesn't sell.' You're accepting their terms. If you want to know what really scares me, it's not the danger; you're right, they'll protect you. It's that you're changing. You wear makeup all the time now and walk around with your ass stuck out like every guy's trying to fuck you. I haven't seen you straight for months. You're depressed. You're malnourished. Own up to it, Lauri, you're not yourself."

Perhaps she was right. I couldn't be myself after pretending to be somebody else for eight hours. Perhaps it was an illusion that I could tuck Lolita into a locker with her costumes at the end of the day.

I wandered through the empty rooms of the apartment trying to capture a sense of the familiar in my surroundings. The place felt foreign to me. I'd lived there for two years, longer than I'd lived anywhere before, yet I hadn't made it my home. I'd used my roommates to assuage my loneliness after stripping. In my room, I'd tried on costumes for the stage. In the living room, I'd choreographed new acts. Sitting in the kitchen, I'd pumped myself with coffee to work up the nervous excitement I needed at the Nudie-Tease.

What if I forgot about the job, forgot about Lamont, and did something for myself? I used to be able to perform certain rituals to calm myself and remember my worth. Meditation was one; dance was another. I'll dance, I thought; I have the

173

apartment to myself. I'll dance wildly and freely, with movements as sharp and hurting and unfit for the stage as I feel.

I drew the curtains in the living room and put a tape of Aretha Franklin's songs on the tape deck. "Give me a little respect," Aretha wailed. I didn't feel the movement yet. Another line of coke would help. "Just a little bit." The coke caused a rumbling in my belly. I began to move. I twirled around in a neat circle. That's what Rebel does, I thought. Loosen up. "R-E-S-P-E-C-T." Without thinking, I bent over and wiggled my hips, another stripper move. Total abandon, I instructed myself. I swung my head around as if it were disconnected from my body. I pounded my feet on the floor. Arching and contracting my back, and dangling my arms like weightless appendages, I danced until the end of the song. And then the thought slipped into my mind that I was dancing like Nina. Which one of us would be the star? The thought repulsed me, as did my naked body jumping and contorting in the name of self-expression. I still felt a pain in my gut, a solitary sensation in an overall state of numbness. Wishing I could cry, I curled up in a ball on the living-room rug. "The masquerade is over," Aretha Franklin's voice had softened.

"I want to feel better," I moaned. "Someone take care of me.

I fell asleep in that position, and that night I dreamed of a wide-open field where the grass grew tall and the ground was moist. I ran barefoot around the circumference of the field, afraid that if I stepped inside I'd be lost among the reeds. I ran around and around until finally I collapsed in exhaustion. As I lay on the ground, I saw an old woman approaching. She walked slowly, dragging alongside her a Styrofoam cooler. It was Grandma. She unpacked her goods, spreading out before me a colorful array of foods. She fixed two plates of identical servings and handed one of them to me. "What are you doing here?" I asked. "Isn't this the Combat Zone?" She shrugged her shoulders and began to eat; she had all her teeth. In the distance we heard a motor, and then men's voices. Grandma wanted us to hide. I said, "Tell them we're soul mates. Tell them that." The noise of the motor grew louder and I woke up.

In the morning, I decided that I'd go to Virginia to visit my family. I'd go right away. With Grandma, more than anyone in the world, I could feel known. Our bond was too deep to be obscured by the creeping effects of my job. With her, I could still feel.

My mother and stepfather had moved from North Carolina to Virginia; Grandma had moved with them. She lived in a four-unit brick apartment building in a rapidly urbanizing part of town. One block away was the Jewish Community Center, over which she agonized. "Should I go there?" she'd ask each time we spoke on the telephone, ready to argue no matter what the response. "They seem friendly, but why should they bother with a nobody like me? They're rich women. I have nothing."

"You could go to the book discussion groups," I'd prod her.

"No," she'd say, "they don't want me. I have nothing."

That she could be left with nothing had been dramatized to her on the street when a young man snatched her purse. In that purse, she'd kept all of the papers that proved her legitimacy: the records of her marriage and annulment, her Social Security card. The purse was retrieved, papers intact, but Grandma's mistrust of other people deepened. She no longer felt safe taking the long aimless walks she'd gone on for years. Instead, she marched circumspectly from her apartment to the supermarket. She saw, through this limitation on her freedom, that she had indeed grown old, and that growing old in America left her vulnerable to any number of dangers. She became obsessed with the desire to put money in the bank, to "have something." By denying herself butter one week, meat the next, air-conditioning in the summer and the use of too much heating fuel in the winter, she managed to save three hundred dollars from her Welfare checks in the course of a year. She bragged of this feat each time I spoke to her. "You see, Lauri, it may not be much, but now they can't push me aside as a poor old toothless woman."

As she greeted me from the top of the stairs, I noticed that she'd aged dramatically in the six months since I'd seen her. The lines on her face were deeper, and her cheeks had begun to sink into the hollows of her jaws. She'd let her hair grow out into a mass of white curls. Though she stood at only four foot nine, her breadth made up for her height.

"Let me look at you," she said, holding me at arm's distance. You're very thin. You don't look good."

"I'm fine," I said.

She clucked her tongue. "No, you look unhealthy. Come, let's sit, and you'll tell me why you don't eat."

We sat at the table, which was set for one. Grandma stored other dishes under the sink. When the family came to visit, she'd dust them off. Her only other visitor was the social worker from the Welfare department, who came twice a year and promised to look into nicer subsidized housing.

"Do you get lonely?" I asked.

"My days are full of activity. By the time I shop and clean and eat, it's nighttime already. Then I read and write. Lately I feel sleepy, so I take naps."

"Don't you want human contact?" I wanted clues about how to be alone.

She thought for a minute, and then said, "In the last few months, I have been contemplative. I need solitude. A great actress once said, 'I want to be alone.' I'm like her. I want to be alone. Not lonely, alone. You see?"

"You say it with more soul than Greta Garbo."

I suppressed my laughter, because I knew that she spoke seriously. The sight of her, a woman in her eighties, smiling sweetly as she recited the sultry words of Garbo, cheered me. I loved her, with none of the doubts or numbness that tested my love for Lamont. The life she lived diametrically opposed

176

the work I did at the Nudie-Tease, and I wanted to bask in it. She lived simply and cleanly, with no pretensions. She still designed and sewed by hand her own clothing.

As I looked at the dress she wore, a simple length of cotton with openings at the neckline and sleeves, and little else in the way of fashion, it occurred to me that even in her retirement she chose to continue the work she'd done all her life. She'd despised her work in the factory, because the work itself, sewing buttons onto garments, had been repetitive, dull, and stultifying. Now, when she didn't have to, she chose to do the same thing. Did this mean that her claim to have separated her self, her identity, from the demeaning labor she performed, was false? Could there be no separation?

I didn't want to believe that. If it was true of her it must be true of me. Troubled by the thought, I went into the bathroom to do the last of my cocaine. It didn't exist, this separation. I would have to quit my job.

When I came back out to the living room, I felt better. Grandma seated me beside her on the couch for a "heart to heart talk." She put on her bifocals to get a better look at me.

"Tell me, are you still doing this job, this striptease?" she asked.

"I did it, on and off, for almost five years."

"And you like it? Your employer is a good man?"

"He's okay as a boss."

"What do you do for him? What is that striptease, exactly?"

"I told you, Grandma. I stood on a stage and took off my clothes. Like Gypsy Rose Lee. You've heard of her?"

"You won't be offended if I tell you a little story?"

"Go ahead," I said, bracing myself.

"When you were a little girl, seven years old, you refused to sing 'America the Beautiful' in front of your class. Do you remember why?"

The story was family folklore. "I didn't think America was beautiful, what with the Vietnam War and segregation."

"Ah, but the real reason was not that. You told it to me that night when I tucked you into bed. You said, 'Grandma, I was scared to sing. I don't have a good voice.' And you will sing now?" she asked gently.

"I can't sing."

"You see, Lauri, you must get to the root of the problem. You're a radical, no? That's the meaning of the word. If you want love, then come home to the people who love you. Don't take off your clothing for strangers; they won't love you. Or else in twenty years you still won't sing. And you have a beautiful voice, Lauri darling."

Tearful, I leaned my head on her shoulder. She began to hum a Russian folksong she'd sung to me when I was a child. Age had cracked her voice; it had been beautiful. I knew the words, although I didn't understand them. I wished that I felt free enough to sing them.

"Then you will quit this job?" she asked when she'd finished singing.

"I'll quit as soon as I get home," I promised.

With that task done, she went into the kitchen to prepare food, warning me, "You're not going home so skinny."

For the next two hours, I feasted on potatoes, sour cream, noodles, cream, berries, and cake. I felt bloated and alive for the first time in months.

Before I left, Grandma asked me if I smelled gas in her apartment.

"No," I said, afraid that she'd switch into one of her suspicious moods.

"I smell it at night. Do you think they could be pumping it into my apartment? Accidentally, I mean."

"No, Grandma. There's no gas. Don't worry."

"I told the neighbors. I was afraid, you know. I shouldn't have. They might talk to the gas company. They could shut off my gas."

"They won't do that. No one wants to hurt you."

"Maybe you're right," she said uncertainly.

She rode in the car that night when my stepfather drove me to the Greyhound station to catch the midnight bus back to Boston. It was an icy night, with storm warnings all the way up the coast.

"Don't go tonight," she pleaded.

"I have to." I felt anxious to get back to Boston to straighten out my affairs. At the same time, I felt uneasy about leaving. The wind made our small car swerve on the highway. Since our talk, I'd been crying on and off, unused to allowing my emotions such free expression. I felt both sad and exhilarated.

"I'm scared about leaving," I said.

"Nothing will happen to you," she assured me.

"I don't know what I'm going back to, and I'm afraid I'll never be able to come back here."

"I've had that feeling before trips," my stepfather said.

That night, my bus skidded off the highway in Maryland. I awoke to the shouts of a child who'd been flung against the seat in front of her. I suffered only a two-hour delay in my trip, but in the violence of the bus's departure from its course, I saw my own life.

When I returned to Boston, I asked Preston to take me off the schedule at the Nudie-Tease.

"For how long this time?" he asked.

"Indefinitely."

TEN

I AM SINGING

After buying three grams of cocaine, I had five hundred dollars left in the bank. My first task was to find another job. I sat down at the typewriter to write a résumé. Last place of employment? I'd worked at the Nudie-Tease Nightclub for four years. Skills? I could disrobe with style and hustle drinks indefatigably. References?

I looked up at the mirror over my desk. It had served as my measure of employability for all these years. Now it told me nothing. It reflected a face with dark circles under its eyes and lines of worry across its forehead. It was a pretty enough face. But for what purpose? And why bother to have firm breasts and shapely legs if no one would see or touch them?

I wished that Lamont would see me again. If I could feel his hands on my body, I would have reason to feed and clean it. Without him, I didn't want to eat or sleep. I only wanted to snort cocaine. When my stash ran out, I didn't know what I'd do.

Finally, I called him. "I quit the Nudie-Tease."

180

"For two weeks?"

"For good. Will you see me?"

"I don't know," he said. "We've been up and down so many times already."

"And I've always been stripping."

"The place does make you crazy."

"Only me?" I asked.

"You haven't changed."

I started again. "Try me, Lamont. I'm crazy, but I'll get better."

We spent the next few weeks in relative bliss. Instead of fighting, we took day-trips to parks and beaches, deserted in winter. In the evenings, we spent the money left over from my last few weeks at the Nudie-Tease. At night, we kindled more passion than we'd known in a year. I looked at Lamont and marveled that my appreciation of his beauty could have faded. I touched him with the sense that I had gotten back a treasured gift. I wanted to inhale the air around him so deeply that if he left me again I'd still possess his scent. When he said that I was "so fine," I heard his voice and not the voices of anonymous men at the Nudie-Tease. I felt loved.

I knew that my happiness masked a furtive anxiety. I felt it in the morning before I did my first line of coke. I'd wonder what I'd done to deserve such happiness, and if it would be taken away from me. In the back of my mind, I knew that I had to look for work, and that my supply of coke would run out. Then how would I avert my anxiety? I used the drug to feel good; as long as I stayed in good spirits I could keep my man, and as long as I had him, I felt good.

Biology presented an answer to this dilemma, although I was slow to recognize the symptoms. First my breasts swelled; Lamont noted their growth with approval. Then fatigue set in; no amount of coke or caffeine seemed to revive me. When my menstruation lasted only two hours, I finally went for a test.

181

"Your test is positive," the man at the laboratory said. "You are pregnant. If you decide that you want an abortion, we can refer you to a clinic."

"No," I said, "this is the answer."

"I beg your pardon?"

"I want to be pregnant."

With a baby inside of me, I couldn't do drugs. I had to nourish the fetus rather than poison it with chemicals. Now I had a reason to clean up my act. To hell with paid jobs; I'd be a mother. Lamont would never leave me if I mothered his child. He'd suffer through an unpleasant week or two while I withdrew from cocaine, knowing that my crankiness was a trade-off for the health of our child. I could even forget about being sexy for a few months, because pregnancy exempted women from judgment.

I didn't want to tell Lamont right away. I knew that the decision to become parents involved more than biological exigencies. I was afraid that he might not want the child; he had less at stake if he opted for abortion.

For a week, I kept the pregnancy a secret. With the knowledge of its presence, I experienced a euphoria unlike anything I'd felt on drugs. The tingling and fullness in my body seemed to extend beyond my own flesh. The world was pregnant. Food existed to nourish expected offspring. Houses came equipped with cribs and diapers. I looked at other women and thought, Are they pregnant? Do they know it yet? I smiled knowingly at women in their last trimester of pregnancy. In a maternity shop, I fingered the garments I couldn't afford to buy. I sat on the floor of a bookstore reading about natural childbirth.

I wondered if Lamont knew. Each time he passed his hand over my belly, I thought that he must. He commended me on the abrupt termination of my coke habit. My growing appetite surprised him. He explained away my tiredness as a natural adjustment reaction to unemployment; he felt the same way, he said. Warmed by his empathy, I vowed to tell him the truth the next day.

We were to meet in a Mexican restaurant at seven in the evening. I arrived on time and ordered a glass of milk. As I waited for him, I planned the scene. I'm pregnant, I'd say. His face would break into a smile of pride and amazement. He'd squeak out the words, We're going to have a baby? I'd nod. He'd propose marriage.

He still hadn't arrived by seven-thirty. I ordered another glass of milk, wishing he could be on time just once. He invariably showed up late, if at all, mumbling some feeble excuse. If I challenged him, he'd turn around and leave. Or he'd say, "If you don't want to wait then don't." By seven-forty-five, my stomach felt tight. I thought I might vomit the milk. Why didn't I leave, as he would?

At eight o'clock, as I resigned myself to the fact that I'd been stood up, he ambled into the restaurant. His squinted eyes told me that he'd been smoking marijuana. His walk was slack and his lips were tight. I hated him in this state. He became like a stranger, his reactions unfamiliar to me. He'd laugh if I said something serious or snarl if I tried to be affectionate. He might walk off, leaving me alone on a dark street at midnight, or try to make love to me in a movie theater. I'd try to penetrate his narcosis, to provoke some familiar response, even if it was anger, jealousy, or disgust.

"Where were you?"

He grinned. "I took the dogs for a walk in the park. Then I got to talking with some dudes."

"And I'm supposed to wait for you, whenever you show up is fine?"

"I don't care what you do." He started to leave.

"Lamont, I've got to talk to you." I spoke firmly, with no pleading in my voice. We had to talk business now; the fantasy didn't exist.

183

He slumped into a chair. "The bitch is back. I thought she went on vacation."

"Very funny."

We ordered and ate in silence. I stared at him, wishing it was in my power to amputate the unpleasant parts of his personality. I'd preserve his core, which I knew and loved, while trimming away the damaged extremities. If he wasn't in pain, he wouldn't lash out at me.

The food brought him down. "What do you want to talk about?"

"I'm pregnant."

"You're pregnant." He tried out the words in a solemn voice. Then, jubilantly, "You're pregnant!"

"Three weeks."

"Three weeks pregnant," he echoed in an almost reverent tone. "It's mine?"

"Come on. I haven't been out of your sight for a month."

"It'll be a beautiful baby," he mused, stroking his beard. "I kind of like the feeling, knowing I could make you pregnant."

"So you've got sperm. What do you want to do about it?"

"I don't know," he said more soberly. "I have to think about it. Ask me in a week."

"Can't we talk about it?"

"No; no, we can't."

I started to cry. He said, "Eat some more. Aren't you supposed to eat when you're pregnant?"

For the next week, I hated everything that reminded me of pregnancy. Post-menopausal women were in their prime. I pitied pregnant women their distended, misshapen bellies. At the same time, I envied them the marriages that made the births of their babies plausible. I deplored my femaleness, which had gotten me into this predicament. With wry humor, I thought that I'd finally used my sex, the one qualification my job had called for, and in doing so had made myself unemployable. And not only in the Zone; I recalled Vita's experience of being shuffled from job to job while she carried her son. It would be a matter of months before the visibility of my abdomen made me subject to the same treatment. I'd thought that pregnancy would introduce automatic and positive change into my life, that I'd be cared for and protected. It didn't work that way, apparently. I felt more vulnerable than ever, and I felt furious at the fetus in my womb for holding out a false promise and then betraying me. All week I starved it. I spent the remainder of my money on cocaine, more concerned with fending off my own depression than with guarding the baby's well-being. The "baby" was a time bomb growing inside me. The nausea that gagged me in the mornings and the fatigue that overwhelmed me throughout the day signaled its malice.

I waited for Lamont's response, although I knew that to have a baby with him would be sheer lunacy. In my paralysis, I began to focus again on the Nudie-Tease, where nothing changed and nothing happened, where women portrayed an eighteen-year-old sexuality until they were "over the hill," and where pregnancy didn't exist. I knew what to expect there. It was safe; it was controlled. The uncertainty of my present condition, the daily changes and growth of the fetus, terrified me. I couldn't control them. I wished someone would. I prayed that someone would step in and take charge of my life.

Lamont and I talked on Sunday. "Why don't you go away until May," he suggested. "While we're apart, we can decide what to do about the baby."

"But then I'll be five months pregnant. There won't be a choice."

"Oh."

Twice in one day, I arranged and canceled appointments at an abortion clinic. On my third try, the woman said, "Are you sure?"

"No."

"Well, come in and we'll talk about it. You have to be clear about it before we'll perform an abortion."

185

On Tuesday morning, my roommate awoke me with a phone call from my mother. She had never called me before. She must know.

"How are you?" she began.

"So-so." I had her attention now; I wanted to give her the details of my life slowly, allowing her time to reconstruct it piece by piece. "I'm feeling a little bit sick. Lamont and I have been fighting."

Softly, she said, "I have some sad news. Grandma died last night."

I felt like I'd been struck.

My mother went on. "She had a stroke. She went quickly."

"No no no no no NO!" I kept repeating.

"Her neighbors called the police. She had told them she smelled gas. You know, her fears. That's why the police came and found her," my mother's voice broke, "on the bathroom floor. I went there."

"Oh, my God."

"And I cleaned the feces. They shouldn't see her that way."

For an instant, I pictured my mother in this last act of tenderness toward her mother. I imagined her guilt in having been unable to ease the fears, unable to give her mother a family, a refuge from danger. In Grandma's world, the only safety was in books.

"You did all you could," I said.

"She wouldn't let me help her. What a waste, the divided world she lived in."

"When will the funeral be?"

"There won't be one. Her body will be cremated tomorrow. Don't come home for it; there's no use."

I hung up the phone and ran out of the house screaming, "No!" Without stopping to put on a coat, I ran down ten blocks to the river. My fingers turned red and then white. The houses and the air looked as gray as the old snow. I didn't know where I went. The sun went down. I was back at my apartment. My body began to ache as it thawed. The person I would have turned to for comfort was dead.

The next day, the day of Grandma's cremation, I went back to work at the Nudie-Tease. I was there, I told myself, to earn money for an abortion.

"I knew you'd be back," Rebel greeted me in the dressing room. "Can't keep you away."

"I'm only working four days," I told her.

"Is that right?" She took out her vial of coke. "Want to do a one-on-one? Best blow this side of Miami, I'll swear by that."

My mouth watered at the sight of it. "What's it going for?"

"Cheap. One hundred a gram. Here, try some."

Hungrily, I lifted the silver spoon to my nose. As the cocaine dripped back into my throat and melted into my saliva, I savored the numbness it created. I'd used up the last of my stash. Maybe I'd work a few extra days to buy a couple of grams, just enough to get me through the abortion.

"I don't suppose you noticed the marquee when you walked in," said Rebel, with a slight swagger in her voice. "Rebel Rawlins, up in lights."

"Congratulations! Now you're happy?"

"I tell you, if it's not one thing it's another. I got to share the glory with two other girls. Preston and them decided one star's not enough. Now they want three, all on the same level."

"So you'll have company up there, Rebel."

"I'm aiming to get rid of those other two."

Finding Rebel unchanged was somehow comforting to me. I looked at her tall frame, with the muscular legs that sent tremors through the audience as she strutted across the stage. Her hair, dark brown and meticulously groomed, swept dramatically across her shoulders. The entire room reeked of her perfume. She presided over the dressing room, sending other dancers scurrying to fetch her coffee and to inform the DJ of her preference for all front-stage shows. She'd reached her summit, and I couldn't imagine her anywhere else.

My grandmother had died, I was pregnant, my relationship was in shambles, but there still existed in the world of stripping a promise of glamour and perfection, an image of womanhood uncompromised by changes in the real world. In the Nudie-Tease, I did not need to feel pain. In timelessness, death became an impossibility. Lolita could not get pregnant, because she was a strip*teaser;* her relations with men were never consummated. She was a perpetual child whose innocence many men wished to protect, albeit for profit and lust. Everything was fine in the Zone. The economic recession did not prevent the men from buying seven-dollar drinks for the show girls. The witnesses of violence against a few unfortunate men were not deterred from returning to see the beautiful women spread their legs. They shouted and applauded; some cursed and masturbated. The money poured in. The women looked lovely, and felt nothing, and that was all.

Leaving the Nudie-Tease the night before my abortion, I came across three men standing around a drunk.

"He's dead," one man said matter-of-factly. "Froze to death."

"No," said another. "I saw him breathe."

"Ought to be dead," said the third man. "Scum of the earth."

When they'd walked on, I went to see for myself. The man was breathing, almost imperceptibly. Bending closer, I saw that it was J.B., a man I'd known from the Nudie-Tease, about three years back. I'd met him when he'd just gotten out of prison. He'd been twenty-five years old then, and had spent the last seven years behind bars. If he'd messed up while on parole, they'd send him back. One day, some guys had jumped his brother, and J.B. had gone looking for them with a knife. They'd found him first and had knocked out all his teeth. He'd come to the Nudie-Tease a week later, looking like an old man; he'd had no money for dentures. I'd given him fifty dollars.

When I'd gotten out of work that night, I'd seen him on the stairs of the subway station, drunk, bloodied, and crying. I hadn't wanted to leave him there for the cops to find, but I'd known I couldn't help him. I'd sat at the bottom of the stairs and cried with him. Now, three years later, he lay frozen on the pavement. That's the best way to die, I thought, frozen and feeling nothing; he'll be taken to the morgue, scooped up and taken to the morgue. I walked on to the subway. A policeman stood on the corner. It wouldn't hurt to tell him, I decided.

"There's a guy lying frozen on Washington Street."

"Oh, yeah?" said the cop.

"He's alive."

"Okay, lady, we'll check it out." And he stood there.

In the morning, Lamont and I went together to the clinic. He had agreed to go through the abortion with me. He took no financial responsibility for it, and I could not control his emotional response. Insisting on his attendance was my way of ensuring his involvement. I didn't want to go through it alone.

Before leaving the house, I did as much coke as I could without making my heart race. I ignored the literature the clinic had sent me explaining "the procedure," preferring to put myself in the hands of medical experts. Just as pregnancy had "happened" to me through no will of my own, so the abortion would be done to me. Through passivity I would elude pain.

"It's cold in here," I complained to the physician's assistant as I lay stretched out on the examining table. My legs hung from stirrups and my hands gripped the edges of the table. The coldness of the metal and the air made me shiver.

I felt the pinprick injection of the local anaesthetic into my cervix and heard the doctor's calm voice explaining, "Now we'll insert the plastic cannula, to dilate your cervix. There will be some mild cramping."

Starting as a centralized spasm in my abdomen, the cramp-

189

ing spread crablike through my torso and down my legs. It grew in intensity as it grew in area. My entire body jolted with the unexpectedness of the pain.

"Push down on my stomach!" I screamed to Lamont.

"That's not safe." The doctor pushed his hand back.

The pain ruptured my numbness. As the force of suction began to vacuum out the contents of my womb, it also pushed me out of my torpor. The fetus passed in front of me as blood in a tube, the machine whirred and gnawed at my insides, and for the first time in years I knew that what I felt was real. It demanded the involvement of my nerves and my muscles, my thoughts and my feelings. As my uterus clamped down around the plastic tubing, there appeared in my mind a flood of images: I saw Grandma rushing into her bathroom, mistaking her final pain for a pain like any other, something to be flushed and discarded. I saw Charlene being beaten by some man. I saw myself, dressed as Lolita, trying to pull Grandma from her paranoia, to tell me that she would not leave me. I wanted to curse her for deserting me now. I saw Lamont as a young boy who had been brutalized daily by his father, and who asked, really without knowing, Will you love me? I saw the safety for him in loving a woman who was also afraid to feel. I saw Lolita sitting in a classroom trying to articulate the emptiness she felt when men told her she was beautiful. I thought of Rebel's spirit and Vita's tenacity, and saw a fleeting image of them as white and male, walking out of the Nudie-Tease with their jaws set for success. I saw the fetus as a baby, emerging after nine months into the hands of my great-great-grandmother, Chaya Sarah, the midwife of the village Bolshoi Tokmak in the Ukraine, one hundred years ago. I felt the ripping of the tissue from my womb, and as it issued from me, I knew beyond a doubt that there could be no separation between what I did and who I was. There was only me, who felt raw and hurting, but fully alive. As the cramping began to subside, I saw that as in its intensity there'd been pain, in its abatement there was relief. Feeling had its rewards. I had chosen to survive by involving myself in my own pain.

In the next few days, I saw that I had other choices as well. I could continue to work at a job that numbed and hurt me, or I could look for other work. Likewise, I could choose to improve or leave my relationship with Lamont; I could stop blaming myself for his problems. I would not die without a man, although I might feel lonely at times. Most important, I wanted to sustain the aliveness I'd discovered without re-creating the pain that had sparked it.

I decided to spend the next semester in New York. To Lamont I explained, "If there's anything left for us, let's pick it up when I've figured out what I'm about."

He agreed, "Something's got to give."

"I thought it would revolutionize my life, quitting the Nu-die-Tease, but I need other changes."

When I returned to the club later that week to pick up my costumes, I knew that I'd left stripping for good. This resignation differed from the others because I could see beyond it.

The Combat Zone had changed since I'd first forayed into it with B. B. Jewel in 1976. The Twilight Lounge was gone, replaced by a "Live Nude" establishment, where scantily clad women sat in cubicles talking into telephone receivers to the men who peered at them through Plexiglas windows. Eight strip joints remained, most of them peopled by hookers, pimps, and johns. Several others had been shut down and boarded over. While a neighboring medical complex and Chinatown merchants sought to expand their boundaries, corporate interests bid for the property. The two-square-block "adult entertainment" district, with its peep shows, dirty bookstores, X-rated cinemas, and strip joints, faced an uncertain future.

In other ways, the Zone remained unaltered by time. Drunks and their wine bottles still littered the streets. The marquees of rivaling strip joints boasted the best-looking dancers in Boston. Pimps hung out at the corner pizza counters;

they rapped their approval on the glass as women walked by. Hookers, identifiable by the tightness of their pants and the garishness of their makeup, waited impassively for customers.

LaGrange Street had always harbored the worst elements of the Zone. Notorious as a pick-up place for hookers, it looked more like an alley than a street. Filthy in the daylight and unlit at night, the street spanned the length of one block. In its one strip joint, the Trap Door, aging strippers served as a backdrop to the activities of solicitation and drug-pushing. Pimps sat at the bar minding their wares. Fights erupted frequently. I'd been down the street only a few times, finding it more difficult to glamorize the Nudie-Tease if I saw the low-life around it. On this day, however, I could think of nothing more appropriate than to see the seamy side of the Zone. So I turned down LaGrange Street.

"What's happening, baby," said a pimp, as I walked by the bar. "Cat got your tongue?"

"You don't want to talk to me," I said. "I'm a square."

"I could turn you out into something nice, girl." He wore gold and diamonds and a smile so gracious. On his left arm he wore a cast. "You work down here? Hey, come here. What's your name?"

I brushed by him. Looking down at the ground, I walked straight into a hooker.

"Watch it," she said in a druggy voice.

Lifting my eyes from her emaciated legs, to her bare arms covered with needle tracks, to her generous breasts and her uncombed hair, I almost fainted.

"Charlene."

"Here I am," she said noncommittally.

"What are you doing here?"

She looked at me vacantly. "Same old thing, except now I'm on the street."

"But you're hooking."

"I got my customers in the club, till Preston fired me. They

192

paid better in there, to be with a dancer after hours. Now it's a hustle and Ajax is breathing down my neck."

"Your pimp?"

She nodded. "You just talked to him. He likes you, Lolita. He liked me, too, at first."

"When was that?"

"I don't know. A few years."

The pieces began to fall together. "Then he started beating you, and you hid it. You talked about Charlie like he was some kind of angel. How come, Charlene?"

She looked at me with a childlike, dreamy expression. "I wanted someone to love me like my daddy did. He was good to me, before he left. Charlie was like that."

"Then you did know Charlie."

"I knew him, one time. I didn't make him pay. He was sweet to me."

"Listen, my name is Lauri. And yours is Sue." I wrote my address and telephone number on a slip of paper and handed it to her.

"You're different from me," she said.

"Not so different."

"Will you say hi to all the girls for me, Lolita?" She folded her arms in front of her, as if to hide them. "Tell Preston I could work again, I'm not drinking so much. Don't tell him where you saw me. Please? It's cold out here. I'm going in."

She walked back up to the Trap Door slowly, on legs as thin as stilts. Her hips, which had once sloped outward on a gentle arc, had lost their shape. Her hair looked limp and straggly. When she turned back to wave at me, I realized that I was looking at a woman whose spirit had left her, but whose body could still be sold. I saw the slip of paper I'd given her lying on the ground, and I picked it up, lest it fall into the wrong hands.

Inside the Nudie-Tease, my eyes took a moment to adjust to the darkness. I remembered the concurrent shock and acceptance with which I had greeted the surroundings that had emerged out of the Twilight Lounge five years earlier. In some ways what I'd seen there had mirrored what I'd seen in the world, and it hadn't surprised me. Women dressed and undressed to accentuate their sexual attractiveness. Men and women who had never met before shared flirtations and intimacies. In the strip joint they exchanged cash for sexual pleasure, or the illusion of sexual pleasure; on the outside, decorum and emotional complexities veiled that exchange. Some people worked while others profited from their labor. For reasons colored by prejudice and money hunger, employers valued certain workers more than others. At the age of sixteen, I had barely perceived these matters; yet, their presence in my everyday life had allowed me to slip into "the life" without suffering a complete rupture of my values. At the Nudie-Tease, a veneer of legitimacy and glamour had disguised the unpleasantness. And as the boundaries of the strip joint had gradually encroached on my life, my sense of the normal had converged with what I'd seen around me at work. Now, I took for granted the parading of naked women down the T-shaped runway. The Bare Beaver Bar no longer shocked me with the crudity of its name; it was simply the back room of the Nudie-Tease. When customers said, "Show me your pussy," or "How much do you cost?" their comments seemed as innocuous to me as "Where is the toothpaste?" might seem to a clerk in a drugstore. That is what I must fight, I told myself as my eyes became accustomed to the darkness. As long as I had the ability to see, I must use it, inside and outside the Combat Zone.

I went into the dressing room to collect my costumes. They'd be of no use to me now. Perhaps I'd save them to wear on Halloween, when women who'd never dream of going near the Zone took the liberty to dress up as strippers and prostitutes. Maybe I'd find a kinky boyfriend who'd enjoy my black garters and fishnets. Or I could return my rags to Goodwill, where I'd found them.

A young dancer stood at the mirror primping herself. She wore a flashy costume consisting of a red sequined jumpsuit and a black cape.

"It's brand new," she said. "From Desiree."

"So you want to be a star?"

She looked aghast. "You don't know who I am? I'm Raquel. My picture's out front, alongside Rebel's and Farrah's. You must be new here."

"I'm old. Sorry I didn't look at the marquee. I just came by for my costumes because I'm quitting the business."

"Let me see what you've got," she demanded. "Maybe I'll buy something off of you."

"I wouldn't touch them with a ten foot pole." Rebel had entered the room.

Raquel stiffened into a defensive posture. ' You want them yourself, Rebel?"

"You better take a look at them, honey, before you make any offers," Rebel snickered. "Lolita never did make it onto our best-dressed list."

"I'm bigger than you, anyhow," Raquel said to me as she strutted huffily out of the dressing room.

Rebel flashed an inimical look in the direction of the closing door. "That girl's only sixteen years old."

"She'll be a hit."

"Don't let her baby face fool you. She's no virgin."

"Neither are we," I said.

"Speak for yourself. I'm as clean as the day I was born. I don't let this place get to me."

"What are you going to do when you leave here?" I asked. "Do you think about it?"

"I don't waste time on worrying." She took out her hand mirror and razor blade.

"You can't keep this job past the age of thirty-five, tops. Then what?"

"I'll get married, and I'll do it in white, because I got nothing to be ashamed of and nothing to hide. My own mama watched me on the stage here. There's nothing dirty about it."

"Where is your mother?"

"They fired her and wouldn't say why." Rebel angrily slashed at the coke she'd poured onto the little mirror. "I wish I could give her everything she never had. I know one thing. She's not going back down to Georgia to work in that mill, if I have to strip ten days a week." She held the mirror out to me. "You want some?"

"No thanks. I went straight."

"One of these days I will, too," she said as she leaned down to do a line. "Come a day I won't be able to smell a flower or some sweet perfume."

"Don't let that happen. It's not worth it."

"I'll tell you something: It's already happened." She sat quietly for a moment, a pose inconsistent with her usual defiance. Then she got up to dress for the stage.

On my way out of the bar, I went to say good-bye to Vita. She had been out of work for a few weeks. She looked thin and sick. While the management had stopped harassing her as blatantly as before, they had not given her a raise or a promotion; and she still had not pushed her way into a radio station.

She was eating a hamburger. On the table in front of her were two others, plus a milkshake.

"Trying to gain weight?" I asked.

"You got it. You should try it, too."

"I don't need to now. I came back here to say good-bye. I quit here for good."

She looked at me until I began to squirm. "Can I trust you with a secret? This isn't one of those dancers' secrets you go squealing to the next person who comes along. I have a child who could be taken away from me for this."

"You can trust me."

"I'm going to be a stripper. Not here in Boston, where people know me. I'm getting booked up in Maine. I'll be a novelty up there; they don't see too many black people."

"You must be kidding. It's against everything you believe."

"I need the money, pure and simple. I can't make ends meet, and I can't get Welfare as long as I'm on the payroll. I have no intention of seeing my son go hungry. My first child died. That's not going to happen again. So I'm eating until I have enough meat on me to show."

"You're a beautiful woman, Vita, and they don't care what you look like."

"I really believe you're leaving for good this time," she said. "I have a favor to ask you."

"What's that?"

"Can I borrow your costumes? You're about my size."

I shoved the bag at her. "Here, keep them."

She lifted the microphone out of its holder to announce the next dancer. Turning to me, she said, "Don't be a stranger. You've got my number."

I spent the next few months in New York. I lived in a loft in SoHo and spent much of my time in the Library of the Performing Arts at Lincoln Center. There, I read everything I could find about burlesque and striptease. I wanted to know how other people analyzed the life I'd just left. I found little in the way of analysis. Over the decades, newspapermen had reported the scandals and thrills of stripping as if they were something deliciously naughty and amusing. Ex-strippers had written fond memoirs in which they bemoaned the lost days of glory for the profession. In the library's selection, I found little that spoke to my own experience.

During that time, I also read the notebooks Grandma had left for me. With an even hand, she had copied passages from the works of many of the world's greatest thinkers. The works of Tolstoy, Turgenev, and Chekhov appeared first in Russian and then in English translation. Using juxtaposing quotations, she compared Buddha to Aristotle, and Jesus to Luther. Freud, Nietzsche, and Kant all had their places in her notebooks. She quoted sparingly at times, extensively at others, always choosing passages with an optimistic bent and an inquisitive tone. An awe and love of knowledge itself bound together the disparate quotes she chose.

Hidden in the back of one of the notebooks, I found a composition that Grandma had written in 1965, entitled "On the Eve of My Retirement." In this sole piece of writing, she gave voice to her own perceptions. Written with the sadness of a life of missed opportunities, the essay ended with a plea to "mankind" to continue to search for knowledge, and to condemn no one to the isolation of being misunderstood.

As I read these words, an understanding of the woman who had written them crystalized for me for the first time. I pictured her in the apartment she'd rented in 1965, a small room in Brooklyn, near the ocean. She sat at her table, a woman who had many fears, and who felt that outside of her room were people who might hurt her. She wrote to these people, whom she called mankind, as if in the telling of her story she would become known, and thus protected. Danger lay in the unknown. What was not known could be misconstrued; it could lead to prejudice and persecution. I saw that the vigilance with which she sought out and wrote down the revelations of other scholars resembled the desperation of her search for knowledge of others' intent to harm her. These two pursuits of knowledge did not reveal a split in her personality, but rather represented different aspects of her way of being in the world. Ignorance of any sort would bring harm. Ironically, when she died, her neighbors thought to call the police because, in her fear, she had told them that she smelled gas in her apartment. Perhaps in a different world she would not have been so isolated. Perhaps she would have felt more certain of her chances for psychic survival without constructing an ever-present evil to discover and expurgate. As it stood, she had been a troubled person, complex but undivided.

It would take me a long, long time to reconcile myself to her death. I felt a loss that reached deeper than the emotion I felt for her, to a core region of my self, in which I both believed and doubted that my life would have meaning. I had always turned to her for that assurance. Now I had myself, in the process of healing, and I had the memory of her.

Back in Boston several months later, I met Patrice on the street. She looked spectacular, with her black hair loose and her cheeks red from the sun.

"I've been thinking about you," I greeted her. "I quit the Nudie-Tease a few months ago."

She smiled at me and began to talk in her familiar, racy manner. "Funny I should run in to you today. I just went to audition for a part in a play about strippers. I thought, This is a tailor-made role. The director told me I had talent, she'd like to use me in some other show, but that I clearly had no sense of what a stripper is like. Shit, what was I doing for all those years in the Zone?"

"Trying to play every other character but the stripper. I was doing the same thing." We looked at each other and laughed. "What are you doing for money nowadays?"

"Waitressing. It's the same old shit, stripping or not stripping. There's a war going on all over." Her eyes lit up, and she raised her voice for dramatic emphasis. "In the Zone, it's like free fire, open range. That's where the troops go in, the common foot soldiers. That's where the paratroopers are diving into the burning cities, instead of just doing the paperwork that orders the ammunition that loads the guns that someone else shoots. But across the street from where I live there's spray-painted on a building, 'A woman was raped on this block.' Now I have a little bit of choice which unit I fight in. There's no such thing as a conscientious objector in this war. It's just condensed in the Zone."

"And dangerous," I added. "Out here I feel like I've got a chance."

Patrice looked down at the ground. "Have you seen Charlene?"

"She got out. But she may have been better off before."

"I wonder," said Patrice. Then, "It's good to see you. And we'll stay in touch."

Over the next few months, as I looked outward for explanations of my experiences, and as I joined in various political struggles, I also looked inward. I realized that in her search for knowledge, Grandma had recognized the power of words, while silencing herself. In my life, I could break that silence. By recounting my years as a stripper, I assert my strength and my wholeness. I am singing.